For a Glory and a Covering

FOR A Glory AND A Covering

A Practical Theology of Marriage

Douglas Wilson

canonpress
Moscow, Idaho

Published by Canon Press
P.O. Box 8729, Moscow, ID 83843
800-488-2034 | www.canonpress.com

Cover and interior photography by Mark LaMoreaux.
Cover design by Laura Storm and Lucy Zoe Jones.
Cover design inspired by the poem *Vineyard of En Gedi*, written by Douglas Wilson, *Untune the Sky: Occasional, Stammering Verse* (Lancaster: Veritas Press, 2001). Printed with the magnanimous consent of the fine folks at Veritas Press from whom you should buy some books.

Library of Congress Cataloging-in-Publication Data

Wilson, Douglas, 1953-
  For a glory and a covering : a practical theology of marriage /
Douglas Wilson.
    p. cm.
  ISBN-13: 978-1-59128-041-5 (alk. paper)
  ISBN-10: 1-59128-041-9 (alk. paper)
    1. Marriage—Religious aspects—Christianity.   I. Title.
BV835.W565 2006
248.4—dc22
                                          2006027395

09 10 11 12 13 14 15 16 17 18   9 8 7 6 5 4 3 2

For the four households,
and all the others to come.

Contents

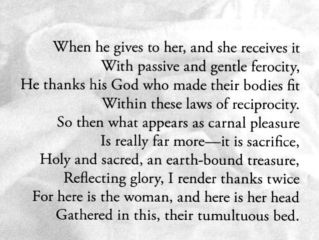

When he gives to her, and she receives it
With passive and gentle ferocity,
He thanks his God who made their bodies fit
Within these laws of reciprocity.
So then what appears as carnal pleasure
Is really far more—it is sacrifice,
Holy and sacred, an earth-bound treasure,
Reflecting glory, I render thanks twice
For here is the woman, and here is her head
Gathered in this, their tumultuous bed.

Vineyard of En Gedi
Douglas Wilson

Preface

I began my second book on marriage, *Federal Husband*, somewhat apologetically:

> Anyone who undertakes to add to the number of modern books on marriage had better have some good reason. This is particularly true if the author in question is doing for the second time and all apparently unprovoked. One would think our interest in marriage books would be waning by this time; like the woman in the gospels, the more our doctors treat us, the worse we get.

But as the years go by, I become less apologetic for repeating myself. This newest book began as a series of sermons for the saints at Christ Church in Moscow, Idaho. The reason for yet another set of messages on this subject was a pastoral one. As our church had grown significantly in numbers, we have wanted to go over the importance of godly marriage regularly. And as our children have grown up and married in our midst, we recognize they may not remember the messages that were preached when they were in junior high. We have consequently seen a constant need to repeat certain things over again: "To write the same things to you, to me indeed is not grievous, but for you it is safe" (Phil. 3:1).

At the same time, while it is important to go over certain principles repeatedly, there is a danger to this as well. That danger is to simply repeat verbatim what has been said before, and in the same way it has been said before. After a little bit of that, the saints will be begging for messages on supralapsarianism. So what I have sought to do here is develop more detailed applications for some of the principles set down in *Reforming Marriage, Federal Husband* and *My Life for Yours,* and to do so in a way that explicitly grounds those principles in the nature of our triune God. Those who have read the previous books will encounter some echoes, but nevertheless there is a large amount of new material here. Those who have not read the previous books should be able to read this one as a stand-alone treatment of biblical marriage.

Of course, I have to thank God for Nancy. She is the kind of wife that makes it possible for a man like me to write a book on marriage.

Introduction
Why This Book Might Not Do You Any Good

Marriage is instituted by the triune God, and when rightly understood it is one of the most glorious pictures of the gospel ever given to man. And of course, when it is abused (as it often is), it presents a potent false gospel as well. That false gospel either seduces people into a sentimental mess, attracting them on false grounds and with false promises, or it presents an unwelcome caricature that causes people to be repelled. But as Christians who want to structure all of our lives on the bedrock of the Scriptures, we should certainly do the same with marriage, and we will quickly discover that this way of living presents the world with a *stark* alternative.

> Marriage is honourable in all, and the bed undefiled: but whoremongers and adulterers God will judge. Let your conversation be without covetousness; and be content with such things as ye have: for he hath said, I will never leave thee, nor forsake thee. (Heb. 13:4–5)

The author of Hebrews tells us that marriage is an honorable state and that marriage does not somehow become dishonorable because of the marriage bed—a thought that some with prudish tendencies might be tempted to embrace. Marriage is honorable, and the bed is undefiled and undefiling. This does not mean the marriage bed cannot be defiled, for God will judge those who defile marriage by means of adultery or other forms of immorality.

Having said this, he goes on to say that our "conversation" (i.e., our way of life) needs to be free of covetousness (v. 5a). It is not an accident that this exhortation immediately follows the verse on marriage. Be *content* with what you have, he says—and this includes the spouse you have been given. God will never leave or forsake us (v. 5b), and that is grounds for comfort and contentment.

So why begin our discussion of marriage here? We can easily see how discontent leads to certain obvious sins, including sins that can plague a marriage. For example, a man's discontent can breed lust, causing him to violate the tenth commandment by desiring another man's wife. Or discontent can breed financial disaster and debt-slavery, which in turn places a great deal of pressure on a marriage. But these are not the central reasons I want to begin this book on marriage at this point. The great problem with discontented people (and that means discontented husbands and wives) is that they are the most *unteachable* people on earth.

It is important therefore for us to begin all our considerations with this basic lesson. All of us must thank God for our condition and estate: "Giving thanks always *for all things* unto God and the Father in the name of our Lord Jesus Christ" (Eph. 5:20). "Giving thanks for all things" is one of the prerequisites for understanding *anything* that St. Paul says in the following verses about marriage between a man and a woman, or between Christ and the Church. The one thing that discontented people cannot do is give thanks, and therefore they cannot have the wisdom that contentment brings.

Very often, discontented married people are former discontented *unmarried* people. In other words, discontent is very rarely fixed by rearranging the furniture or by walking from over here to over there. Wherever you go, *there you are*. And if you are unteachable, marriage does not alter what you are, but rather amplifies what you are. If you are discontented, marriage will provide you with little more than newer and more complex ways of getting into sin.

There are three kinds of unmarried adults. The first are called to that station by God and are uniquely gifted for it. The apostle Paul was in this category (1 Cor. 7:7). Almost by definition, contentment is not an issue here. The second group consists of those who are dealing with a hard providence, such as single parents. They want to be married, and they don't like being unmarried, so the temptation to discontent is very real. The third category consists of lazy people who need to get off the dime. The problem here is a spurious discontent—being discontent with all the lack of potential spouses out there. (But as we consider these categories from a distance, let us be careful to mind our own business—we shouldn't be trying to assign every single person we know to a particular category.) My primary exhortation is for those in the second category. Often unmarried people in this station are afraid of contentment "because if I get content with my condition, then God will make me *stay* this way, and because I am content, I won't *care* anymore!" But remember that being discontented is like taking ugly pills, and they are addictive—you will find yourself still taking them even after you get married.

The word of the Lord is this: If we are discontent in our marriages, we are not capable of learning anything fundamental about marriage, and the more we refuse to learn, the more we *think* we know, because we have all kinds of "stories." The irony is that today so much material on marriage is actually used (whether the authors or seminar speakers intend this or not) to inflame *discontent:* "Lord, here am I. Change *him.*" And if someone calls us on our own discontent, we will display that unteachable spirit mentioned earlier: "The Scripture doesn't apply here"; "He doesn't know my situation." But God does know your situation, and He is the one who inspired St. Paul to introduce his teaching on marriage by saying that we should give thanks for *all* things.

Marriage is a glorious thing, and this truth has ramifications. There were two aspects of the Israelite camp in the wilderness that ought never go together: the Shekinah glory in the sky and the grumbling on the ground. Far too many Christian marriages are like that. Husbands and wives complain and moan in the midst of glory, in the very shadow of stupefying glory.

Another reason couples do not profit from teaching on marriage is their confusion of letter and spirit. We have seen how discontent is a universal corrosive and how those who are discontent *cannot* learn to live biblically in the married state. But discontent is not the only sin in the world, and we have to consider a few other reasons why many professing Christians might not be able to learn what it means to be a godly husband or wife. We are not yet building the house of marriage; we are simply trying to get the foundation lines straight.

> Do we begin again to commend ourselves? or need we, as some others, epistles of commendation to you, or letters of commendation from you? Ye are our epistle written in our hearts, known and read of all men: Forasmuch as ye are manifestly declared to be the epistle of Christ ministered by us, written not with ink, but with the Spirit of the living God; not in tables of stone, but in fleshy tables of the heart. . . . Seeing then that we have such hope, we use great plainness of speech. (2 Cor. 3:1–3, 12)

There is a basic principle here that has a profound application to marriage. Paul doesn't need to commend himself (v. 1), because the Corinthians already are that commendation (v. 2). The Corinthians themselves are written, not with ink, and not in tables of stone, but in the fleshly tables of the heart (v. 3). Paul trusts in God for all this and not in himself at all (v. 4–5). God has made him a minister of "the new testament; not of the letter, but of the Spirit." And this is the point where he says the Spirit gives life *and the letter kills* (v. 6). Now if the glory of the older testament was too glorious to look at, and *it* was temporary (v. 7), how much more will the ministry of the Holy Spirit be even more glorious (v. 8)? If condemnation is glorious (rightly understood), how much more will the ministry of righteousness be glorious (v. 9)? The glory that came makes the older glory seem inglorious by comparison (v. 10). The old was glorious, the new even more so (v. 11). This being the case, the apostles used "great plainness of speech" (v. 12).

Now what does he mean when he says the "letter kills"? Paul is clearly *not* arguing against ever writing things down, for his argument that the letter kills and the Spirit gives life is an argument that he himself wrote down. *The issue is therefore not "the letters" in themselves.* The issue is not paper and ink. Paul is addressing a hermeneutical issue—do we interpret words in the power of the Spirit, or do we just blunder clunkily through the literal meanings of some of the words, sharping and flatting as we go? Rightly understood by faith, the older covenant was glorious. Wrongly understood, the letters were letters of condemnation, and those letters were letters of death. Rightly understood by faith, the New Testament realities are far more glorious. Wrongly understood, the higher the letters go, the greater the fall when the Spirit of God does not give understanding. This means that in the time of the New Covenant, the consequences for hearing the Word in a distorted way are far more severe than they ever were in the Old Covenant.

So, how does this apply to marriage? As St. Paul might say, "Much in every way." Those who want to learn how to be married—to be "the wife of a happy husband" or the husband who "loves his wife as Christ did the church"—must understand how quickly the standards involved can turn into a newer, better, and higher *law.* But the law (taken in this sense) only increases and provokes transgression (Rom. 3:20; 5:20). Understood by faith, it of course does not do this, but when the Letter is there and the Holy Spirit is not, the results are condemnation and the very impiety that "the high standards" are vainly trying to keep away. "Standards," including very high standards, by themselves do not provide any power for living up to them. It follows that any "standards for marriage" are powerless in themselves as well.

There are many familial issues that readily fall into this category: headship, decision-making, submission, home schooling, bread baking, domesticity, Christian schools, dress standards, head coverings, entertainment standards, curriculum decisions, and much, much more. As Tom Hovestol once memorably put it, "It struck me that something about rightness is wrong."[1] Conservative Christians have a consistent problem that comes from the desire to "be right," and this includes "being right" on traditional family issues. But as my father faithfully taught me, there is a deeper right than being right. As a marriage counselor, I have seen more than a few marriages in which husbands and wives had "high standards" for Christian conduct, and yet tolerated and advanced amazingly toxic attitudes in the home.

As Paul taught this fundamental principle of Christian living, he was consistently misrepresented as one who was attacking the law itself. This distortion of his position even continues down to the present, and the same thing happens when someone offers any lesser criticisms on the same principle. The conversation goes something like this:

"Excuse me, but I think you are holding that book upside down."

"What do you have against Jane Austen?"

"Nothing, but I think you would get more out of it if you held it right side up."

"Well, I cannot believe the arrogance! What's with your hostility to classic literature?"

Clearly, criticism of holding the book upside down *is not a criticism of the book*. In the same way, pointing out misuses of the law is not the same as attacking the law itself.

This brings us to the need for "great plainness of speech" that Paul mentioned. This particular sin is not automatically impossible just because we live in the New Covenant era. The same patterns of temptation arise again and again in every era, and they afflict us down to the present. The apostle addresses the problem, in talking to New Covenant saints, and he speaks to them bluntly. It's as if he is saying, "You need to get this straight,

---

[1] Tom Hovestol, *Extreme Righteousness* (Chicago: Moody Press, 1997), 20.

and if you do not get it straight, the *higher* the standards you
have for your marriage, the *worse* your marital condition will be.
It's for this reason I use great plainness of speech." The hardness
such pietism causes in marriage requires a jackhammer, not a
feather duster.

The only high standards that are at all spiritually safe are standards that are born from gratitude, thanksgiving, and gladness
and simplicity of heart (Acts 2:46). Grace is foundational, and
so the higher you want the structure to go, the more necessary it
is for that foundation to be solid and straight. From a thankful
heart, all things may be received, including the great gifts of discipline and standards (1 Tim. 4:4–5). But without that gratitude
pervading everything, strict views on marriage will simply create
an earthly hell for yourself and others.

There is a third reason why this book might not do you any
good. The first reason we considered was discontent, because discontented people are profoundly unteachable. The second stum-
bling block is our tendency to trust in the letter of the law instead
of trusting in the Spirit of God. This leads to death, even if the
"law" concerned is made up of a great deal of good advice about
marriage. And we now come to the third major hindrance, which
is the temptation to "fix the other one first."

> Therefore all things whatsoever ye would that men should do to
> you, do ye even so to them: for this is the law and the prophets.
> (Mt. 7:12)

This fundamental orientation that the Lord requires of us is com-
monly called the Golden Rule. The Lord teaches that we should
take whatever we desire to have done for us and use *that* as the
guide and standard for how we undertake to treat *others*. Moreover, He tells us that this *is* the law and the prophets—it sums up
what God requires of all of us in all our dealings with others.

Now let's bring this teaching into marriage. Our problem is
that the husband knows what verses his wife ought to be heeding,

and if we were to ask her, she would probably be able to point out the passages that he is neglecting. In short, when it comes to marriage, we neglect the fundamental biblical demeanor of Christian living. In other words, a man needs to remember that his wife is his *neighbor*, and a wife needs to understand that her husband is her neighbor. To love our neighbor as ourselves is *another* summary of the law and the prophets (Mt. 22:38–40). That husbands should love their wives as they love themselves is the apostle Paul's profound application of this same basic principle (Eph. 5:28–29). The point is that the general principle for all Christian demeanor *does* in fact apply to marriage. How could it not?

All of us are called to love our neighbor as ourselves. The responsibility all of us have as Christians to love others as ourselves and to put the interests of the other person first is a universal responsibility. This means a godly Christian man is of necessity going to be a godly Christian husband, and a godly Christian woman is going to be a godly Christian wife. But when it comes to marriage, far too many Christians believe they have the right to be rude, thoughtless, tacky, bitter, demanding, or angry—as though marital closeness eradicated all responsibility to live as a civil human being. When called on this, we defend ourselves by saying that the *other* one is not obeying the Golden Rule: "*She* started it"; "*He* won't listen." But to do this (and in some cases, even to *see* it) is a violation of the Golden Rule. The rule is *not* to "do unto others as you imagine they are doing unto you."

Many marriages are in bad shape because people assume that good marriages can somehow be separated from a basic godly demeanor throughout the course of our lives. As long as husbands and wives commit this particular error, the words of life with regard to marriage will just bounce off them—like a ping-pong ball off the forehead of a bronze statue.

Another problem is this: Rather than live in the high mountain air of the Golden Rule, mankind has sought out many devices. We alter the words of the Lord, with some of the alterations being just as true as the original, although the overall standard has been adjusted a tad lower. For example, there is a difference between "Do unto others as you would have them do unto you" and "Do *not* do unto others what you do *not* want done unto you." The latter is just fine, and is biblical as far as it goes, but the former expression involves considerably more. You don't want to be murdered, so don't murder—but this, by itself, is too low a bar.

In this regard, C. S. Lewis once commented that men think that love means not giving trouble to others, while women think that it means taking trouble for others.[2] In this difference, the women appear to have the advantage. Men need to learn this: "So ought men to love their wives as their own bodies. He that loveth his wife loveth himself. For no man ever yet hated his own flesh; but nourisheth and cherisheth it, even as the Lord the church" (Eph. 5:28–29). Note what St. Paul is basically saying here: "Husbands, take trouble. Take time. Nourish. Cherish. Sacrifice. *Die.*" Too many husbands imitate a Christ who never took on flesh, who stayed in heaven, leaving us alone. But this is not what Christ did. The Lord Jesus took on flesh, and in doing so, took *trouble* for us.

If husbands underachieve here, wives frequently overachieve. Deep within every wife lurks the heart of a missionary and reformer. The basic orientation of wives is generally healthy; wives are geared toward taking trouble for others, which is the biblical definition of love. But the point of wisdom here is to learn where the brakes are. There is such a thing as excess, even here. Lewis also once described a woman "who lived for others"—and you could tell who those others were by their hunted expression.

A godly marriage does not consist of this marital technique or that one. A godly marriage occurs when a man and a woman both *die to themselves*, and are raised to the life that seeks the best interest of the other in all things. This is the only kind of godly marriage there is. And when we give all away in this manner, we

[2] C. S. Lewis, *The Screwtape Letters* (New York: Macmillan, 1962), 121.

discover that we receive all. We learn to give in order to receive, in order to be able to give some more. And we are married to someone who is doing the same thing.

Now it is not possible to live this way without an applied incarnational knowledge of what the Holy Trinity is like. As we turn away from these sins, we must necessarily turn toward God Himself. And in turning toward Him, we are learning to imitate Him, as dearly loved children (Eph. 5:1). This leads us to the first topic we must consider, which is the connection between marriage and the very nature of God.

PART I:
Marriage and the Nature of God

Marriage, Trinity, and Incarnation

So let us suppose that, by the grace of God, we have repented of our discontent and want to be teachable. We want to hear the word of truth *in* truth, and make applications according to the Spirit and not according to our idea of what the letter ought to have been. We also want to apply whatever we learn to ourselves first and not to our spouse first. Finally, we want to live as married couples *within* the triune life of God. But how are we to understand the significance of God's triune life in our marriages? Consider these two passages:

> And did not he make one? Yet had he the residue of the spirit. And wherefore one? That he might seek a godly seed. Therefore take heed to your spirit, and let none deal treacherously against the wife of his youth. (Mal. 2:15)

> Neither pray I for these alone, but for them also which shall believe on me through their word; that they all may be one; as thou, Father, art in me, and I in thee, that they also may be one in us: that the world may believe that thou hast sent me. And the glory which thou gavest me I have given them; that they may be one, even as we are one: I in them, and thou in me, that they may be made perfect in one; and that the world may know that thou hast sent me, and hast loved them, as thou hast loved me. (Jn. 17:20–23)

Malachi tells husbands that they must take heed to their spirits so that they will not deal treacherously with the wife of their youth, their wife by covenant. God made husband and wife, not for a seed, but for a *godly* seed, and so the *oneness* between husband and wife must be preserved (2:15). In His great prayer of John 17, the Lord Jesus is praying for oneness among all believers. Oneness between husband and wife is just one application of this, but it is a very important application. First, Jesus prayed for this result, and this obviously means that such a result between believing husband and wife is the will of God (v. 20). Jesus wants believers to be one *in the same kind of way* that the Father and Son are one, and He wants us to be one by means of *participation* in *their* unity (v. 21). We are not to imitate the triune unity from a distance. We are to imitate it from within. The result is a powerful statement of the gospel (v. 21). The glory that the Father gave the Son, the Son has given to believers, so that they might be one (v. 22). Christ is in us, and the Father is in Christ, with the result that we are "made perfect" in one (v. 23). Again, the world knows from this that the Father sent the Son into the world, and the world also knows that the Father loves believers just as He loves His Son (v. 23).

In order to grasp this rightly, we first have to grasp a point of grammar: the difference between indicatives (statements) and imperatives (commands). The pattern of godliness in Scripture is to build *imperatives* on the foundation of *indicatives*. God in His word says that something is true. We hear, and believe, and therefore are enabled to reckon in our lives the truth that this is so. We hear, in order to be able to do, by faith alone. Only faith hears this rightly. "You have died to sin in Christ. Therefore, die to sin": this is gospel. "Die to sin, and you will therefore die in Christ to sin": this is false gospel. The gospel is all about what God *has done*, and what we must therefore do as a consequence. "Work out your own salvation with fear and trembling. For it is God which worketh in you both to will and to do of his good pleasure" (Phil. 2:12b–13). We are to work out what God works in, *and nothing else.*

But what is God *not* working in? Too many Christians read this as saying that God is working in "nice" things, and that therefore we are to work out "nice" things. But this is nothing but superficial moralism. We are not told to work out what we think would be pleasant for God to have worked in had we been consulted. We are told to work out our *salvation*, for God is working in us to will and to do for His good pleasure. This transcends the nature of a spiritual backrub—it's more like spiritual boot camp.

So what is He working in? In short, God is "working in" *trinitarian realities.* He is working *Himself* into us. He is our salvation, and He is triune. So what does this mean in marriage? Please remember, again, that the message of this chapter is not telling you what you ought to be working in. This is a description of what God *is* doing in you, whether you ever read a book like this or not. I am urging you to stop fighting it, and I am exhorting you to gladly embrace what God is doing anyway. He is doing it, so just come along quietly. "Work it out" is another way of saying "deal with it."

This is trinitarian glory. We are to understand what God is already doing and then live accordingly. In the married state, we are to *indwell* one another as the Father indwells the Son and the Son the Father (Jn. 17:21). Husbands are to bestow glory on their wives, and wives are to render glory to their husbands (v. 22). Why exchange glory? Why not leave the glory where it was? Why rearrange the furniture? The answer is, "In order to be one as God is one." God is not a static unit with static glory. The triune God is the One in whom there is an eternal and mutual bestowal and receiving of glory. As the Father loves the Son, and has loved us, so husbands and wives love one another (v. 23). We will pursue this further later, but this is Trinitarian imitation—but never from a distance. We do not imitate God from fifty million miles away. God has ushered us into communion with Himself, and so we worship God from within that fellowship.

We should remember that these truths are for all believers, and not just for married couples. But given what Scripture teaches us about marriage, the gospel, and oneness, we know that all these general truths about believers can be manifested in marriage first, in a clearer, more heightened way—marriage is the showcase of Christian unity. This will be made even more evident when we address what Scripture teaches us about the Incarnation.

It is not possible to talk about the Trinity without talking about the one who fully revealed the triune nature of God to us—the Lord Jesus. He is the eternal Word of God, the one who took on our flesh in order to bring us to salvation, revealing the Father to us. This is why the doctrines of the Trinity and the Incarnation must be considered together. In the Incarnation, the eternally begotten Son of God became the son of Mary, and, through her, a genuine son of Adam. This also has a profound impact on what it means to be human, and it cannot help but affect our marriages.

Consider what Paul says about Christ:

> [H]e raised [Christ] from the dead, and set him at his own right hand in the heavenly places, far above all principality, and power, and might, and dominion, and every name that is named, not only in this world, but also in that which is to come: and hath put all things under his feet, and gave him to be the head over all things to the church, which is his body, the fulness of him that filleth all in all. (Eph. 1:20–23)

We are picking up this text in mid-sentence. The apostle Paul has been recording his prayer for the Ephesians, in which he requests that they would begin to comprehend the nature of what had been bestowed on them in Christ. In Christ, certain realities have been given to us as redeemed creatures, and it is possible for these creatures to begin to grasp the ungraspable—by the grace of God. The essence of this gift is that God took a ragtag bunch of sinners and transformed them into the *fullness* of His Son.

There are many truths worth pondering in this text, but the one we need to note here is that Christ is described as the "head over all things to the church," His body, the fullness of Him who fills all things. By becoming a bridegroom, Christ received fullness from His bride, even though He was the one who filled all things. This "dependence" on His bride does not challenge His headship; rather, it is the *basis* for it. In the limited, bounded space of human marriage, how would this translate? "The husband is the head over his house for the wife, to the wife, who is his body, who is his fullness, even though his authority fills the house."

Thinking about this rapidly brings us to the point where thought staggers. We have trouble (understandably) talking about the Trinity "raw." It is not possible for us to grasp what the Trinity is like (by obtaining, say, the schematic diagrams) and then go off and apply that to our marriages. Even though we might say that the Trinity is "logically" prior to the Incarnation, because the Trinity describes the way God is apart from creation or redemption, we cannot "access" the Trinity unless the triune God *reveals* Himself to us, and He has chosen to do this in the Incarnation of His Son. Jesus says that if we have seen Him, we have seen the Father (Jn. 14:6–9).

But there is another step to take as well. God has revealed the Trinity to us *through a marriage*. We learn about the triune God through an understanding of Christ and the Church, but we are also called to understand Christ and the Church by applying what we are taught about *that* to our own marriages. "Husbands, love your wives, even as Christ also loved the church, and gave himself for it" (Eph. 5:25). "As the church is subject unto Christ, so let the wives be to their own husbands in every thing" (Eph. 5:24). We don't really learn anything "raw" in a systematics class; rather, we are to learn everything in what might be called *an incarnational loop*—applying what theology we know results in greater understanding of that theology, which in turn results in better application, and so on.

Of course, I must emphasize that husbands and wives are not called to *duplicate* or *reenact* the precise relationship between Christ and the Church. We cannot do anything of the kind. Husbands are not called to die for their wives as a sinless substitutionary atonement, for example. The emphasis of this teaching is not marital hubris. Nevertheless, we are explicitly commanded to pattern our lives after His example, and we are given many things that we can imitate.

One very common problem is a superficial or thoughtless imitation of Christ's example. We read Ephesians 5, see that husbands and wives are like Christ and the Church, and immediately translate this into a minimal "nice thought for the day": "Husbands, love your wives 'a lot.'" It is somewhat better if we pay close attention to what Christ is described as actually doing in that chapter, and so we see that this involves sacrifice, teaching, nourishing, cherishing, and so on. This is important in its place, but we forget that the entire book of Ephesians is crammed with teaching about Christ and the Church, including the text we have just been considering.

Recall that in our discussion of the Trinity, we talked about mutual indwelling. The Father and the Son are one, for example. They are not one because they have merged, but rather because the distinct Father indwells the Son, and the Son indwells the Father, while remaining fully and completely Themselves. The Spirit indwells the Father and the Son as well; each Person of the Trinity fully indwells the others (without confusion of the Persons). Theologians call this mutual indwelling *perichoresis*. We have the same kind of thing in marriage. Husbands must say, "I am the head of my body, my wife. I am the head of the one who fills me." The wife must say, "I am the fullness of the one who is my head." Anyone who comes away from a careful reading of the apostle Paul's teaching on marriage with the idea that the husband is "the boss" and the wife is "the slave" is someone not to be trusted with *any* text. In his fine book *Trinity and Reality*, Ralph Smith puts it this way:

> [There is a] slander that says because Christianity teaches that man is the head of his home, it permits men to abuse their wives. What the Bible really teaches is very different. According to the Bible, to be the leader means to sacrifice oneself for the other, as Christ sacrificed Himself for the Church. If Christ is the pattern for the husband—and He is—then what the Bible calls for is self-sacrificial love that glorifies the wife. This is not a view that promotes abuse of any kind.[1]

The first chapter of Ephesians therefore helps us to make sense of the fifth chapter. If you come to the fifth chapter with the wrong assumptions about what has been going on, you will be hopelessly overwhelmed by a rigid Marriage Law. If all that Christ's coming did was raise the ethical standard to a higher level, then our condition is hopeless. But if we have received the grace revealed in the Incarnation—the grace St. Paul prayed that we might have in Ephesians 1:17–18—what then? If you have the spirit of wisdom and revelation, how will you think of your husband or wife? If the eyes of your understanding are enlightened, and you know how the saints are a glorious inheritance for Christ, then you know what a husband and a wife are. And you will not know it until then.

---

[1] Ralph Smith, *Trinity and Reality* (Moscow: Canon Press, 2004), 66.

Imitation

It may seem odd to include a chapter on imitation in a marriage book, but it is actually a very important aspect of marriage. In fact, it is so important to godliness in marriage that the world has an entire framework of countermeasures arrayed against it, so that most of us already have prejudices firmly in place. We are individualists at heart, and the world has trained us to mock imitation as necessarily a mindless conformism. We are prepared and set, lest anyone entice us into some kind of obedience.

But consider these scriptural passages that teach imitation:

> Be ye therefore followers of God, as dear children; and walk in love, as Christ also hath loved us, and hath given himself for us an offering and a sacrifice to God for a sweetsmelling savour. (Eph. 5:1–2)

> I write not these things to shame you, but as my beloved sons I warn you. For though ye have ten thousand instructors in Christ, yet have ye not many fathers: for in Christ Jesus I have begotten you through the gospel. Wherefore I beseech you, be ye followers of me. (1 Cor. 4:14–16)

> Be ye followers of me, even as I also am of Christ. (1 Cor. 11:1)

The word that is translated here as "follower" is the Greek word *mimetes*, which means "imitator." This means that when you learn by imitation, you do what the other person is doing. When you learn in the textbook way, you do what the other is saying or writing. There is a place for this, but we don't really need to make room for it. We all know to do this; most of us have spent a lifetime learning many lessons from books. But we do need to make room for the type of imitation required of us in the above texts. In Ephesians 5, we are told to imitate God in the same way that dear children imitate their parents (v. 1), and that means that we are to walk in love sacrificially (v. 2). Well, yes, someone might say, but this is imitation of *God,* not sinful human beings. But this imitation of God is compared to the imitation that children render to parents. We are not told to avoid imitating mere mortals; we are called to it. We are created this way—it is a design feature. In 1 Corinthians 4, the apostle beseeches his Corinthian converts to imitate him (v. 16). Later in chapter 11, he says that he imitates Christ, and he urges the Corinthians to imitate him in his imitation (v. 1).

The elders of the church are told not to be lords over God's heritage, but rather to be examples to the flock (1 Pet. 5:3). St. Paul tells Timothy to set his life, in word, in love, in spirit, in faith, and in purity, as an example to the believers (1 Tim. 4:12). The people of God are told to consider the outcome of the way of life that is set by the leaders of the church (Heb. 13:7, 17). Now why does God give His people all these examples? So that they can *imitate* them. Not only is imitation a godly thing (as defined this way), but it is the way to godliness.

The Greek word for this imitation, *mimetes,* is the root of our word *mimicry.* The difference between learning by mimicry and learning by abstract information transfer is the difference between someone who is fluent in a language and someone who has just memorized the paradigms in the back of their textbook. God has created us to learn this way. You can see it with an adoring two-year-old sister following her masterful four-year-old brother around the living room or up and down the driveway. What he says, she says, a millisecond later—monkey see, monkey do.

This seems like mindless copying, but it is the foundation of all creaturely wisdom.

In Scripture, learning is profoundly incarnational. But we have been taught (in countless ways) that true knowledge is abstract and disembodied. When people begin to self-consciously imitate their parents and their elders, it is not long before the charges of "mind-control" and "cult" begin to fly. Part of the godly fruit of incarnational imitation is like-mindedness, which the Bible praises in a number of places (Rom. 15:5–6; Phil. 2:2, 20), and which our modern world condemns. It is not even hard to find Christians who are wary of like-mindedness. Instead, they say, you have to be an individual. You have to think for yourself. Be your own dog. You must not imitate others, period. The result of this vain exercise (like throwing rocks at the moon) does not eliminate imitation; it only guarantees the imitation of fools.

So how does this apply to marriage? Given the fact that God has made the world in this way, and given that imitation is built into all authority relationships (God/man, parents/children, elders/congregation), and given that marriage is a relationship in which husband and wife are expressly told to model their relationship after Christ and the church, what follows from this?

Because of the closeness of marriage, imitation works both ways. Husbands learn from their wives by imitation, and wives learn from their husbands by imitation. But the initiative and fundamental responsibility for all this lies with the husband. He should be able to say to his wife, with a straight face, "I want you to imitate me in this." Now there are two basic reasons why these words stick in our throats. The first is the propaganda of modernity that we have already addressed. We think about saying something like that, and our minds fill up with imaginary scenarios: "Who do you think *you* are?" But humility does not mean adopting an "aw, shucks" posture. Real humility is doing what God says to do.

But the second reason these words stick in a husband's throat is that these words condemn us. We hesitate to say them for the same reason we hesitate in the middle of the Lord's Prayer. If we ask God to forgive us our debts as we forgive our debtors, then it might appear that we are really asking God not to forgive us at all. In the same way, husbands might rather say, "Do as I say, not as I do." But pressure for some kind of imitation is already occurring. If husbands are selfish and sinful, then that is the closest, living model that his wife has to imitate. If she does not desire to imitate that (and she shouldn't), she is nevertheless swimming against the current—the current that embodied disobedience establishes in every home. If he doesn't want her to imitate him because of his sin, he must recognize that the sin still creates a demand for imitation. So a husband is providing a model for imitation regardless of what he does. His behavior simply controls whether it is a good model or a bad one. The husband and father teaches through the example of his entire demeanor. That demeanor is potent and will result in imitation down to the bone, including what he thinks of as secret sins. But, by the grace of God, his example is potent in the other direction as well.

Because of how God created the world, if a man and woman live together for any length of time, they will imitate one another. The only question is whether this will be done self-consciously for good, as part of their mutual disciplines in sanctification, or in a haphazard way, to the detriment of both husband and wife. If the imitation is being done by two Christians who are self-consciously (by faith) dwelling with one another in peace, and *within* one another by the grace of God, then this imitation will be a profound help for good. This approach of faith will not mean that husband and wife will slavishly copy one another's faults, but rather that they will encourage one another where they are respectively weak and establish one another in love where they are respectively strong. Imitation is not a way to lose our individuality for good—it is part of the gospel pattern by which we receive back what we lose for the sake of Christ. As we imitate one another in this way, we become more truly ourselves.

The Virtue of Jealousy

In the Scriptures, jealousy is a virtue. Like all good things, it can be bent and distorted into sin, but for some reason we have come to think that it is necessarily sinful, which is not the case at all. As a result, we in the modern world are not nearly jealous enough. Our rejection of this virtue of jealousy is one of the ways we have refused to imitate God.

> Take heed to thyself, lest thou make a covenant with the inhabitants of the land whither thou goest, lest it be for a snare in the midst of thee: but ye shall destroy their altars, break their images, and cut down their groves: for thou shalt worship no other god: for the LORD, *whose name is Jealous*, is a jealous God: lest thou make a covenant with the inhabitants of the land, and they go a whoring after their gods, and do sacrifice unto their gods, and one call thee, and thou eat of his sacrifice; and thou take of their daughters unto thy sons, and their daughters go a whoring after their gods, and make thy sons go a whoring after their gods. Thou shalt make thee no molten gods." (Exod. 34:12–17)

Throughout Scripture, idolatry is consistently compared to adultery. The marital image is a strong one, and thus it is not at all a stretch to learn about jealousy in a marital context from the Bible's general teaching about God's jealousy in the presence of idols. In the above text, God prohibits Israel from making covenant with the inhabitants of the land (v. 12). The Jews are to wage total religious war against them, destroying all the instruments of their idolatry (v. 13). The Israelites were to worship no other God but the Lord, and the reason for this is that *His name is Jealous* (v. 14). Single-minded worship of the only God is necessary to prevent "whoring" after other gods (v. 15). The result of this idolatrous worship will be intermarriages, which will result in further liturgical adulteration (v. 16). To avoid this situation, the Israelites were to make no molten gods (v. 17).

Godly jealousy is fierce—the scriptural testimony is very clear on that point. Moreover, the passages that refer to jealousy are overwhelmingly positive, and the fact that our default assumptions about jealousy are negative should tell us something about how unscriptural our worldview has become. As we have seen, God's *name* is Jealous (Exod. 34:14). In the Ten Commandments, God visits the iniquity of the fathers to three and four generations precisely because of His jealousy (Exod. 20:5; Deut. 5:9). We are not to carve images for ourselves to worship because God is a consuming fire, a jealous God (Deut. 4:24). We should fear God and swear by His name (being identified with that name), mindful of His capacity for anger and judgment. Why? He is a jealous God (Deut. 6:15). Joshua knew that the Israelites' "easy believism" would not stand the test of God's jealousy (Josh. 24:19).

The iconoclastic and "unreasonable" Puritan, the Tishbite roaring out of the desert who did not come to initiate "constructive dialogue," and the reforming king who hates idols are all preeminent examples of godliness. This is because in a holy way, jealousy is intractable, righteous, and in many cases altogether terrifying.

But jealousy is also tender. Jealousy is not just given to us as a reaction to a straying wife. It is also portrayed as a glorious motive for redemption. Jealousy is constructive and redemptive as well as being hard as nails. Why will God have mercy on the whole house of Israel? Because He is jealous for His name (Ezek. 39:25). God will show pity upon His people because He is jealous for His land (Joel 2:18). God takes revenge against Nineveh on behalf of His people, because He is a jealous God (Nah. 1:2–3). God spoke comforting words to Zechariah because He was jealous for Jerusalem (Zech. 1:14). God *returns* to Zion because of His great jealousy (Zech. 8:2).

God's prophets and apostles, as imitators of God, had this same kind of redemptive jealousy. When the Lord comes to Elijah, Elijah complains that he had been very jealous for the Lord God of hosts (1 Kgs. 19:10–14). The apostle Paul had the same heart: "For I am jealous over you with godly jealousy: for I have espoused you to one husband, that I may present you as a chaste virgin to Christ" (2 Cor. 11:2).

So what about jealousy in marriage? Scripture acknowledges that jealousy is a very real issue in marriage and is possibly a legitimate concern. In Numbers 5, we find a description of trial by ordeal. This is not a trial in the tradition of some medieval Monty Python send-up. If a man gets jealous of his wife, and he has no evidence, he may bring her to the tabernacle to have her name cleared—or not (Num. 5:14, 30–31). In this case, a "remarkable thing" had to happen in order to convict her. Jesus was quite possibly evoking this law in the famous case of the woman caught in adultery—look at the similarity in the charge, the place of accusation, and the fact that Jesus wrote in the dust on the ground (Jn. 8:1–11).

Because of our negative views of jealousy, we think it is only operative when a couple is on the brink of divorce and a third party is already in the picture. This is often when *ungodly* jealousy starts—but often the couple is in that unenviable position because they were never jealous enough in the full scriptural sense. Godly jealousy should be part of what we are—it is a function of loyalty. God's name is Jealous; this is the way He is, and we should imitate Him. Jealousy is a communicable attribute, and we are expected to have it. Godly jealousy should be insightful, not blind—insightful jealousy sees what no one else is seeing. But so do men with hallucinations—which is why godly jealousy remembers the rules of evidence. Being jealous does not grant us telepathic powers. And we should remember that the jealous one is under authority as well; false accusations cost the accuser (Deut. 22:19).

Godly jealousy is not really about making particular accusations—jealousy builds a fence but does not make assertions about the individuals who don't know why you put the fence there. You can lock your doors at night without accusing every person who walks by of attempted thievery, and you can pull back when someone crosses your "friendly line" without accusing that person of "attempted adultery." Godly jealousy sets particular standards—for friendships, for get-togethers, for business lunches, for entertainment standards, for dress, and so on. Many fathers, for example, are not nearly jealous enough when it comes to how their daughters dress. And they might be surprised at how much it costs to have a daughter look that cheap.

By its very nature, jealousy is possessive, but jealousy goes wrong when it tries to possess things that it has no rightful claim to. The issue is not whether jealousy will be possessive, but rather whether it will be a godly jealousy that is possessive of the right things, or an ungodly jealousy that is possessive of the wrong things or trivial things. A man who is "possessive" of his wife's sexual favors is possessive in the right way. A man who wants to deny other men the right to ever look at his wife's face (which is a common Muslim standard) is being possessive where he has no right to be. There is no indication in Scripture that a husband has the right or responsibility to set that kind of standard. A man or a woman should be jealous over things like sexual infidelity, emotional flirtation, significant amounts of time spent elsewhere when it should be spent at home, money squandered when it should be invested in the home, and so forth. Assuming a balance that rejects the wrong kind of possessiveness, one of the things we must learn in this modern age is the fact that the right kind of possessiveness is a good thing, and that it helps establish real security in the marriage. By cultivating this possessiveness we are becoming like Jesus Christ and His bride.

Marriage and the Holy Spirit

When a man and woman join together in marriage, they are obviously not joined together physically the way Siamese twins are joined. A married man and a married woman are the same biological individuals they were when they were still single. But they are covenantally united—and capable of physical separation. Not only are they capable of such separation, a certain part of their assigned vocational responsibilities requires it. How are we to understand our responsibilities with this in mind?

These things have I spoken unto you, being yet present with you. But the Comforter, which is the Holy Ghost, whom the Father will send in my name, he shall teach you all things, and bring all things to your remembrance, whatsoever I have said unto you. (Jn. 14:25–26)

But when the Comforter is come, whom I will send unto you from the Father, even the Spirit of truth, which proceedeth from the Father, he shall testify of me: and ye also shall bear witness, because ye have been with me from the beginning. (Jn. 15:26–27)

Nevertheless I tell you the truth; it is expedient for you that I go away: for if I go not away, the Comforter will not come unto you; but if I depart, I will send him unto you. (Jn. 16:7)

The Lord Jesus, before He ascended into heaven, instructed His disciples about what He would do in order to deal with the effects of their separation. He was going because He had work of preparation to do.

> In my Father's house are many mansions: if it were not so, I would have told you. I go to prepare a place for you. And if I go and prepare a place for you, I will come again, and receive you unto myself; that where I am, there ye may be also. (Jn. 14:2–3)

The Lord Jesus, the bridegroom, is going away because He has work to do, but the norm is not permanent separation. He will come again and bring us to Himself, so that where He is, we may be also. This is the eternal norm. Christ and His people will be *together*.

But what does He do in the course of the separation? The most significant thing He does, as noted in our texts, is the giving of the Spirit as Comforter. The Comforter will be sent in the name of Jesus, and He will teach and bring to remembrance the things said by the bridegroom while He was on earth (Jn. 14:26). The Comforter will testify of the character of Jesus (Jn. 15:26). And last, there are benefits that will come from this separation that can come no other way (Jn. 16:7).

We have noted numerous times that husbands are to imitate Christ in how they love their wives, but we have also emphasized that husbands are not capable of reenacting certain features of Christ's love (like the substitutionary atonement). Does that not apply here as well? Of course, when husbands are on a two-week business trip, or even if they are gone to work for the day, they are not in a position to "send the Holy Spirit." But although husbands are not to reenact a substitutionary death, they are called to *imitate* a substitutionary death, and though they cannot reenact Pentecost, they are called to *imitate* it. But how?

But let us lay some groundwork first. The Lord tells us that He has made husband and wife one:

And did not he make one? Yet had he the residue of the spirit. And wherefore one? That he might seek a godly seed. Therefore take heed to your spirit, and let none deal treacherously against the wife of his youth. For the LORD, the God of Israel, saith that he hateth putting away: for one covereth violence with his garment, saith the LORD of hosts: therefore take heed to your spirit, that ye deal not treacherously. (Mal. 2:15–16)

God has made husband and wife one, and two times here He commands husbands to take heed to their *spirit*, that they not deal treacherously (unfaithfully) with the wife of their youth.

Now what is the nature of the human spirit in Christ? This is an enormous subject, but the intent here is to show that our relationships are covenantally and organically "active" even when we are around the corner, down the street, and out of earshot. Two married individuals in Christ who are separated are not two isolated marbles, now in different boxes, but rather they are more like two leaves still sharing the same invisible twig. For example, the apostle Paul promises to be with the Corinthians in *spirit* as they take action to discipline a man (1 Cor. 5:3–4). This is not a form of apostolic astral travel, but rather a covenantal reality—"as absent in body, but present in spirit."

Given this covenantal unity, which a husband and wife certainly have, how may a husband and wife practically apply it when they are separated? How may they apply it when they are separated for the day? Or when they are separated for longer periods of time? These applications are necessary at all times, but it becomes more obvious when providence has you apart for extended periods of time.

First, don't sin while apart. Do not deal treacherously with one another (Mal. 2:15–16). And do not sin *together* while apart (Acts 5:1–11).

Second, resolve to do what you can to *impart comfort* in an ongoing way. This is what Jesus has done for His bride—He sends both His Spirit and His letters. The Bible teaches us that news and contact encourage:

> I am glad of the coming of Stephanas and Fortunatus and Achaicus: for that which was lacking on your part they have supplied. For they have refreshed my spirit and yours: therefore acknowledge ye them that are such. (1 Cor. 16:17–18)

In this, think biblically about technological blessings, whether it is email, cell phones, or any other form of communication we might cook up. "As ye also learned of Epaphras our dear fellowservant, who is for you a faithful minister of Christ; who also declared unto us your love in the Spirit" (Col. 1:7–8). A common complaint about certain technological innovations (like cell phones) is that they can result in people walking around in an electronic bubble—separated from all the people they are actually with. This is a problem, but it is a problem of use. The same technology can be used (and should be used) to connect people. Husbands and wives now have a greater capacity to stay connected throughout the day, and they should use it.

Third, *walk in the same spirit*, together or apart: "I desired Titus, and with him I sent a brother. Did Titus make a gain of you? walked we not in the same spirit? walked we not in the same steps?" (2 Cor. 12:18).

And last, *extend a blessing*. A blessing is not just something done by patriarchs on their deathbeds, ministers in the benediction, and by everyone when somebody sneezes. *Bless* one another. Here are some scriptural examples: "Brethren, the grace of our Lord Jesus Christ be with your spirit. Amen" (Gal. 6:18). "The grace of our Lord Jesus Christ be with your spirit. Amen" (Phm. 1:25). A husband at a distance is no less a husband, and no less responsible. When he is on the road, he should *bless* his wife in his prayers. A wife at a distance is no less a wife and no less a blessing. In this, as with everything else we do, we are being conformed to the nature of God.

Reciprocity

We have seen that being a godly Christian husband or wife is a subset of being a godly Christian in general. This being the case, we also see that certain characteristics (that all Christians should have) have a particular and pointed application to husbands and wives. So with this in mind, we need to take a look at some of the "one another" exhortations of the New Testament and apply them to marriage. Of course, for those who are unmarried, these characteristics apply differently, but they still apply. Moreover, if these "one anothers" apply to all believers everywhere, then how much more do they apply within Christian marriage?

> And be not drunk with wine, wherein is excess; but be filled with the Spirit; speaking to yourselves in psalms and hymns and spiritual songs, singing and making melody in your heart to the Lord; giving thanks always for all things unto God and the Father in the name of our Lord Jesus Christ; submitting yourselves one to another in the fear of God. (Eph. 5:18–21)

The central command here is to "be filled with the Spirit." The things that follow are descriptions of what it looks like when someone is filled with the Spirit. The results of this filling are (1) expressing yourself with spiritual music, (2) giving thanks for everything to the Father, and (3) mutual submission to one another. In the verses that follow, the apostle Paul goes on to apply this in a distinctive way to husbands and wives, but what he has said thus far applies to all Christians generally. All Christians are to be filled. All Christians are to sing psalms, hymns, and spiritual songs to themselves and others. All Christians are to be thankful for everything. And all Christians are to submit to one another. This means that there is a sense in which both husbands and wives submit to one another, and the Spirit enables them to do it musically and thankfully. A husband's authority over his wife and a wife's particular submission to her husband are a subset of this broader Christian duty for all believers to be filled with the Spirit and to be mutually submissive to one another.

The greatest Christian virtue is love. The Scriptures tell us again and again to love one another: "Owe no man any thing, but to love one another: for he that loveth another hath fulfilled the law" (Rom. 13:8). Love within marriage is the fulfillment of the law and the prophets. "For, brethren, ye have been called unto liberty; only use not liberty for an occasion to the flesh, but by love serve one another" (Gal. 5:13). Love within marriage is the basis of mutual service. "But as touching brotherly love ye need not that I write unto you: for ye yourselves are taught of God to love one another" (1 Thes. 4:9). The need to love one another is obvious—God Himself teaches it to us. "Seeing ye have purified your souls in obeying the truth through the Spirit unto unfeigned love of the brethren, see that ye love one another with a pure heart fervently" (1 Pet. 1:22). The love within marriage is to be pure, unfeigned, and *fervent*. "For this is the message that ye heard from the beginning, that we should love one another" (1 Jn. 3:11; see also 3:23; 4:7; 4:11–12; and 2 Jn. 5). This love is not an optional "add-on"—it is the basic Christian message. Among the virtues of faith, hope, and love, the greatest is love. That we must love one another is the command that fulfills the law and all the prophets. This love is fundamental, foundational, and liberating.

But love excludes certain things. When love is present, we stop doing certain things to "one another." This is another way of recognizing that "one another-ing" is inescapable. The alternatives are not "love one another" or "leave." If we do not love one another, we will sin against one another. What do we do sinfully, negatively, when we are not loving one another? All the "one anothers" that follow are the antithesis of love. "Let us not therefore judge one another any more: but judge this rather, that no man put a stumblingblock or an occasion to fall in his brother's way" (Rom. 14:13). When we do not love, we judge others and we stumble others. "But if ye bite and devour one another, take heed that ye be not consumed one of another" (Gal. 5:15). If we are not feeding and nourishing one another, then of necessity, we are eating and devouring one another. "Let us not be desirous of vain glory, provoking one another, envying one another" (Gal. 5:26). When we do not love, we compete, provoke, and tear down. "Lie not one to another, seeing that ye have put off the old man with his deeds" (Col. 3:9; cf. Eph. 4:25). When we do not live in the love of the truth, we *lie*. "Speak not evil one of another, brethren. He that speaketh evil of his brother, and judgeth his brother, speaketh evil of the law, and judgeth the law: but if thou judge the law, thou art not a doer of the law, but a judge" (Jas. 4:11). If we will not speak what is good to our spouse, and of our spouse, then the alternative is speaking evil.

This does not mean we must embrace a sentimentalist's view of marriage that assumes every good marriage will be free of evil. Sin occurs in marriage, and sin threatens us in our marriages. Keeping in mind all the other principles in play, what are we to do about it? "Walk worthy of the vocation wherewith ye are called, with all lowliness and meekness, with longsuffering, forbearing one another in love; endeavouring to keep the unity of the Spirit in the bond of peace" (Eph. 4:1b–3). Our first option for dealing with sin is thus simply *forbearance:* "Forbearing one another, and forgiving one another, if any man have a quarrel against any: even as Christ forgave you, so also do ye" (Col. 3:13). A close companion to forbearance is forgiveness: "But exhort one another daily, while it is called To day; lest any of you be hardened through the deceitfulness of sin" (Heb. 3:13). This verse teaches that we should also exhort one another continually. Paul teaches the same virtue using a different word: "And I myself also am persuaded of you, my brethren, that ye also are full of goodness, filled with all knowledge, able also to admonish one another" (Rom. 15:14). When we have stumbled, admonition can be a kindness. It should also lead us to confession: "Confess your faults one to another, and pray one for another, that ye may be healed" (Jas. 5:16a).

We will then be able to receive, edify, and comfort one another. "Wherefore receive ye one another, as Christ also received us to the glory of God" (Rom. 15:7). "Wherefore comfort one another with these words" (1 Thes. 4:18). "Wherefore comfort yourselves together, and edify one another, even as also ye do" (1 Thes. 5:11). We can also stir each other up: "And let us consider one another to provoke unto love and to good works: not forsaking the assembling of ourselves together, as the manner of some is; but exhorting one another: and so much the more, as ye see the day approaching" (Heb. 10:24–25). Exhorting and stirring up should be linked with compassion and kindness: "Finally, be ye all of one mind, having compassion one of another, love as brethren, be pitiful, be courteous" (1 Pet. 3:8). "And be ye kind one to another, tenderhearted, forgiving one another, even as God for Christ's sake hath forgiven you" (Eph. 4:32). "Be kindly affectioned one to another with brotherly love; in honour preferring one another" (Rom. 12:10). This is how Christians are called to live.

We can readily see that "one another" is an important scriptural category. And when a man and woman marry, the need to function in terms of these "one another" commands is one of the most obvious things about their relationship. If they pay attention to how Scripture instructs them in this, they will be blessed beyond measure. But if they do not, then they will soon discover that there is no such thing as "leaving one another alone." He who does not gather scatters (Mt. 12:30; Lk. 11:23).

PART II:
Marriage is for Men and Women

What *is* Marriage?

What *is* marriage? On a subject like this, solid definitions are very important, just as false definitions are very threatening. But as we define, we must take care that we do not define as good little abstractionists. Biblical knowing, *especially* concerning marriage, is not a rarified exercise; it is practical and embodied.

> And the LORD God said, It is not good that the man should be alone; I will make him an help meet for him. And out of the ground the LORD God formed every beast of the field, and every fowl of the air; and brought them unto Adam to see what he would call them: and whatsoever Adam called every living creature, that was the name thereof. And Adam gave names to all cattle, and to the fowl of the air, and to every beast of the field; but for Adam there was not found an help meet for him. And the LORD God caused a deep sleep to fall upon Adam, and he slept: and he took one of his ribs, and closed up the flesh instead thereof; And the rib, which the LORD God had taken from man, made he a woman, and brought her unto the man. And Adam said, This is now bone of my bones, and flesh of my flesh: she shall be called Woman, because she was taken out of Man. Therefore shall a man leave his father and his mother, and shall cleave unto his wife: and they shall be one flesh. And they were both naked, the man and his wife, and were not ashamed. (Gen. 2:18–25)

In the course of His creation of the world, God repeatedly calls His creation "good." But when He comes to the solitary male, He says it is *not* good (v. 18). It is not good that man should be alone. God looks at the solitary male and says to Himself that He is clearly *not* finished. Immediately after this, God brought all the beasts and birds to Adam to see what he would call them, and Adam had the privilege of naming the animals (v. 19). But in the process of naming all the animals, Adam found no helper suitable for him there (v. 20), meaning that Adam clearly shared God's sentiment that it was not good for him to be alone.

And so the Lord God threw Adam into a deep sleep, removed a rib from his side, and closed the flesh back up (v. 21). God took that rib, fashioned it into a woman, and brought the woman to the man (v. 22), and then we find the first recorded words of man (v. 23, "Bone of my bones . . ."), and, as Robert Rayburn has helpfully observed, they are a poem, a poem concerning his wife.[1] Then follows an (apparent) decree from Adam concerning the marriages of all his descendants: a man will leave his father and mother, cleave to his wife, and they will be one flesh (v. 24). And the man and wife were both naked and unashamed (v. 25).

In contrast to the earlier situation, this setup was good. The creation was filled with goodness. When God created the light, it was good (1:4). When He created the earth and sea, it was good (1:10). When He fashioned the reproducing herbs and trees, it was good (1:12; 2:9). He made the sun and moon, and it was good (1:18). He filled the oceans and sky with teeming fish and birds, and it was good (1:21). When He made all reproducing animals, after their kind, it was good (1:25). The gold in the earth was good (2:12). Viewing all of it, God said that it was all *very* good (1:31).

But we need to notice the strong element of separation in all this goodness. Light divided from the dark was good (1:4); God divided the earth from the water, and it was good (1:9); the herbs

---

[1] From a talk at a family conference in Sandestin, Florida, in the fall of 2004.

and the trees dividing (after their kind) was good (1:12); God made the sun and moon to divide the light from darkness, and it was good (1:18); God made the fish and birds to divide (after their kind), and it was good (1:21); finally, He divided the animals after their kind also (1:25).

But Adam was unitary, undivided, and alone. So God put him into a deep sleep and divided him into two pieces. God then took the second piece, made it into a woman, and brought her back to him in order to heal the division. God made one into two in order to change those two back into one. In a trinitarian world, unity divided and division unified are good. The two alternatives to trinitarian unity in diversity and diversity in unity are not pleasant to consider—they are (1) unity, period, or (2) fragmentation, period. This is a poor choice indeed, and yet it is the only choice that unbelieving thought can present us. Either we have the monolithic unity of Parmenides or the fractured whirl of Heraclitus. We either have the false unity of modernity or the equally hollow diversity of postmodernity. The only way out of this impasse is Christ.

St. Paul develops this theme in the New Testament:

> For the man is not of the woman; but the woman of the man. Neither was the man created for the woman; but the woman for the man. . . . Nevertheless neither is the man without the woman, neither the woman without the man, in the Lord. For as the woman is of the man, even so is the man also by the woman; but all things of God. (1 Cor. 11:8–9, 11–12)

For just as the first woman was divided from the first man, so every man since then has first been divided from his mother. Before the first woman could be united sexually with the first man, she had to be divided from him. Before any man since that time can be united sexually with a woman, he has to be divided from a woman.

In short, marriage as difference and unity is woven into the nature of all creation and is consistent with it. Man has no authority to defy it. Man can *name* what God has done, but man cannot get God to name what man has done, or is trying to do, in his own name. Legislatures or courts can decree that men can now start marrying men, and those institutions can also, while they are at it, decree that water will start flowing uphill.

So what then is marriage? Marriage is a form of death in separation and resurrection in union. When God created the world, He immediately set about fashioning the world by means of division. He separated man into male and female and pronounced it all very good. But He divided for the sake of richer union, and not for the sake of division itself. What is the principle of this kind of union? The answer is covenant—specifically, covenantal *partaking*. The bond that ties division and union together is a covenant bond; marriage is based on covenantal realities. "But I would have you know, that the head of every man is Christ; and the head of the woman is the man, and the head of Christ is God" (1 Cor. 11:3).

Here we should note that in St. Paul's language, "head" does not mean "boss." Headship is a covenantal category, and an essential aspect of covenant living is covenant partaking or fellowship (*koinonia*). There is no such thing as a boss over *here* commanding someone else over *there*. Covenant headship bridges the division and accomplishes union. Those men who browbeat their wives are setting everything upside down. Authority is the principle of union, not the principle of separation. Authority (biblically understood) is what brings them together.

This means that every husband partakes of the headship of Christ, Christ partakes of the headship of God the Father, the woman partakes of the headship of her husband, and all of this happens in the same covenantal way. In other words, marriage is defined by *partaking*. As we realize this, we can see that the statement about headship in 1 Corinthians 11:3 is actually the hinge of a long argument that began in the previous chapter. The

Israelites partook of Christ in the wilderness (1 Cor. 10:1–5), and they partook of idols in the rebellion (10:6–11). The Corinthian Christians partook of Christ in the Lord's Supper (10:16–17). The Old Testament priests partook of the sacrifices of the altar (10:18). Gentile pagans partook of the table of devils (10:19–22). None of this happens metaphysically, but rather covenantally (10:23–33). The grace involved should not be understood as some kind of magic. St. Paul says that he is a "partaker" by grace (10:30), and then he breaks off his discussion of the Lord's Supper and resumes it in 11:17. But it is crucial to note that in his discussion of men and women and role relationships in 11:3–16, he is not changing the subject for a brief moment. *He is not changing the subject at all.* This is all about partaking.

Just as Christ partakes of the Father covenantally (11:3), so men partake of Christ and women partake of their husbands. This is obviously not the only kind of partaking possible (for example, both men and women together partake of Christ, as in Gal. 3:28), but all partaking is some kind of covenantal partaking.

We have seen in all these examples that covenantal partaking is built into the very structure of the world. This means the world is not divided between those who partake and those who do not partake. Rather, it is divided between those who partake righteously and those who partake unrighteously. We cannot go anywhere to opt out of partaking altogether. For example, a man can partake of his wife (Eph. 5:31) or of a prostitute (1 Cor. 6:16), but in either case, he is partaking. And if he rejects women entirely, he is partaking of the doctrine of demons (1 Tim. 4:1–3).

This said, we have to ask what the preconditions are for covenant partaking in marriage *for blessing*. The first is that you must have an explicit covenant surrounding a sexual relationship. Not everyone who is sexually united is married, and not everyone who has exchanged vows with another is married. The covenant exists when the two elements are there together: covenant vows surrounding a covenant union. The second precondition is the grace of God. Remember that St. Paul said that he partakes by grace (1 Cor. 10:30), and the grace of God manifests its presence in our lives by means of the fruit of the Spirit. The third precondition is clear awareness of the assigned roles that God has given to husbands and wives respectively, particularly in worship. This relates to the question of worshipping God "covered" and "uncovered," which we will address shortly in our discussion of marriage and worship.

In God's pattern, in God's way, glory increases as it descends. In Christ, the one who has descended the furthest, all the glory of the Godhead is revealed. Man bears the image of Christ, and woman bears the image and glory of the man. Conversely, this glory is revealed though submission. Christ submitted to the glory of the Father, men submit to the glory of Christ, and women submit to the glory of a husband who is doing this. Of course, once we come over to this side of the Creator/creature divide, we have to deal with husbands and wives who are in revolt against this cascading glory. Remember that such revolt does not eliminate the partaking, but it does eliminate the blessing of partaking. Further, it incurs the judgment of a jealous God, who hates it when husbands and wives tempt Him.

We live in a man-centered age, and consequently we often miss the entire point of God's warnings. We think that the judgment on our marital sin is the mere "judgment" of an unhappy marriage, and that death (at least) would end that. But many husbands and wives really need to consider their ways and live. How many husbands will come under the judgment of Christ for how they neglected these things during the course of their marriage? Did they live as though Christ were their head? How many wives will have to answer for how they stumbled their husbands and families? Did they live as though their husbands were the head?

The chief end of marriage is the same as the chief end of man—to glorify God and enjoy Him forever. The chief end of marriage is not to have "your needs met." The chief end of marriage is not to get your husband "to finally see." It is not to get your wife to be more responsive. The chief end of marriage is to glorify God and enjoy Him (on His terms) forever.

So we have seen that the creation of man, male and female, is not unrelated to God's pronouncement that the whole creation was "very good." But the same thing is true of the *new* creation in Christ. In the new creation, the relation of husbands and wives plays an important part in the worship of the church, and, conversely, the right worship of God plays an important role in our marriages. This connection helps us understand Paul's discussion of worship in relation to his discussion of partaking and headship. "For a man indeed ought not to cover his head, forasmuch as he is the image and glory of God: but the woman is the glory of the man" (1 Cor. 11:1–16).

St. Paul begins by urging imitation of him, just as he imitates Christ (v. 1). He then urges the Corinthians to "keep the ordinances" that he had delivered to them, indicating that this is apostolic teaching, and not just "a cultural thing" (v. 2). Then comes verse 3, which we have already considered. Consequently, when a man prays or prophesies with head covered, he dishonors his head, that is, Christ (v. 4). And when a woman prays or prophesies while uncovered, she dishonors her head, that is, her husband. She might as well shave her head like the dissolute Corinthian prostitutes did (v. 5). If a woman is going to dishonor her husband, she might as well go whole hog (v. 6). A man ought not cover his head because he is the image and glory of Christ, and a woman ought to cover her head because she is the glory of man. Note that both actions (covering and uncovering) are exhibitions of glory (v. 7). For man did not come from woman, but rather woman from man (v. 8). And the man was not created for the woman, but the woman for the man (v. 9). This is why a woman should have the sign of authority on her head—because of the angels (v. 10). But no one should conclude from this that St. Paul is saying that men and women can be independent of one another (v. 11). Though woman came from man, all men since that time have come from women—and from God (v. 12). *Think* about it, St. Paul argues. Even nature says that long hair on a man is shameful (vv. 13–14). And when a woman has long hair, it is a glory and a covering (v. 15). And if anyone wants to argue about it, St. Paul says, this is the way the church worships (v. 16).

We do not believe these instructions were given to us by the apostle so that we could set them aside as "merely cultural." There are, of course, some cultural adjustments to be made from the ancient world to the present; for example, in our culture, the servants do not wash our feet when we arrive as a guest at someone's house. This is because we wear shoes or boots, not sandals. In our culture, the servant (or, much more likely, the host or hostess) takes the coats. But in this passage, St. Paul appeals in the course of his argument to the very nature of things, and not to the current Greco-Roman milieu.

As we work through this issue, it is quite possible you may still differ for reasons of conscience—perhaps your own conscience, or the conscience of your husband and father. If that is the case, please continue your own practice, and we trust that no one will hassle you for it. May God give us all more light. But we need to address this because it is important to our treatment of marriage, and because we do not want to sidestep an important text on role relations between men and women.

As we address the question of women, marriage, and worship, we have to talk about head coverings. As we do, there are several practical things to keep in mind here. First is that the woman's hair is given for a covering (v. 15), which is why I believe that an additional cloth covering (or hat) is unnecessary. But second, for women to wear an artificial covering is of ancient usage in the church, and if the fundamental realities are remembered, there is nothing wrong with it—wearing a cloth covering is not prohibited. Third, we need to remember that *long* and *short* are comparative terms—but this does not make them meaningless terms. And fourth, the ordinance, however we interpret it, does not apply to women and men generally; it applies to men and women in worship, specifically during the time of prayer and prophecy.

John Newton wrote a wonderful hymn that alludes to this passage (and one other passage) in a wonderful way, tying together what is almost certainly an important allusion by the apostle. The hymn is "Glorious Things of Thee Are Spoken," and the relevant lines are "For a glory and a covering, / Showing that the Lord is near." The prophet Isaiah, speaking of the times of the New Covenant, refers to the Shekinah glory (the glory that used to accompany Israel in the wilderness):

> And the Lord will create upon every dwelling place of mount Zion, and upon her assemblies, a cloud and smoke by day, and the shining of a flaming fire by night: for upon all the glory shall be a defence. (Is. 4:5)

The NKJV translates it this way: "For over all the *glory* there will be a *covering*." This is what Paul is referring to—a godly wife is to her husband what the Shekinah glory was to the tabernacle. Now this is how it all ties in with our foundational theology of marriage, and what we believe marriage actually *is*. The Bible teaches that a woman is the glory of her husband. She is his crown: "A virtuous woman is a crown to her husband" (Prov. 12:4a). And a man does not walk down the street kicking his diadem in front of him in the hopes of making himself look better or more important.

Now, however we interpret this passage, we should be careful to make the glory of the woman central to it. The point is not to hide women, or make them look dowdy, or to put them in the back of the church as though we were embarrassed of them. Women are the glory of their husbands, and that glory should be as obvious as a pillar of fire by night. It needs to be as obvious as a circlet of diamonds around his forehead. As I read this passage, a Christian wife is to wear her hair in a way consistent with beauty and a gentle and modest demeanor. That demeanor honors her husband, and by so doing she becomes the honor of her husband. A woman is the crown of her husband, and the crown goes on the head, in a position of honor. She honors him, and in so doing, she consequently receives great honor.

But notice we have raised the stakes. How would biblical obedience in this instance be slandered and caricatured? If we were really living this way, it could never be that "those Christian men browbeat their wives." A more plausible slander would be that Christian men *glorify* their wives to the point of encouraging vanity. Let us not fall into that sin of vanity—but we should be careful to live in a way that provokes the slander.

Masculinity and Femininity

Talking about how men and women differ from one another ought to be commonplace, but in our egalitarian age, to point out differences that used to be as obvious as the differences between salt and sugar is to be guilty (in some quarters) of a thought crime. Happily, because of advances in neuroscience, this is starting to change, but we still have a great deal to recover and learn.[1] The point is that there is no way to talk about marriage intelligently without addressing *masculinity*—how men are different from women. A corresponding truth would be *femininity*—how women are different from men. But the central concern here is not biology (male and female), or how modern science is now discovering what all of us knew already, but the broader scriptural question of masculinity and femininity.

"But I would have you know, that the head of every man is Christ; and the head of the woman is the man; and the head of Christ is God" (1 Cor. 11:3). This is a text we have already considered, but we need to pursue its ramifications further. We have seen that the passage is talking about a covenantal hierarchy—the Father is the head of Christ, Christ is the head of man, and the man is the head of the woman. But we should also note that headship entails authority (in the biblical sense). This authority which takes responsibility sacrificially is the heart of masculinity.

---

[1] See, for example, Steven Rhoads, *Taking Sex Differences Seriously* (San Francisco: Encounter Books, 2004).

In the human race, these categories of masculinity and femininity are incarnate in male and female, but this is not the only place they are incarnate. Consider how this language of masculinity and femininity applies in various settings. This is not a dualistic principle (some kind of *yin* and *yang*), but rather a hierarchical, layered, and trinitarian reality. Someone can be masculine in one relationship and feminine in another. This is because masculinity is authority, sacrifice, responsibility, and initiative, and femininity is submission, obedience, gratitude, and responsiveness. To the extent that someone is legitimately in authority, makes sacrifices, and takes responsibility and initiative, that person is being "masculine." To the extent that someone submits, obeys, expresses gratitude, and responds to initiative, such a person is being "feminine." We are not to look deep inside ourselves to try to find masculine and feminine "essences," but rather we are to accept our created natures as a given, from our bones out to our skin, and then learn to see how these natures are to relate to one another holistically and obediently.

So, let's see how this plays out. God the Father is masculine with regard to God the Son. Remember that we are taught to call Him "Father." And God the Son is described as being masculine toward us, His bride, the Church. He is the Bridegroom, and we are the Bride. And remember here that a good half of the Bride is made up of males. The Church, though half male, is still corporately feminine. In marriage, the man is the head of the woman, and so in this relation, he is masculine and she is feminine. But take this one step further—imagine a godly Christian mother facing down a defiant, two-year-old son. She is female, he is male, but is that the end of the story? Not at all. She is masculine in this relation, and he is feminine. The source of the trouble in this instance may be the fact that he does not want to be feminine.

God the Father is *not* male. God is a Spirit and those who worship Him must do so in spirit and in truth. This alone should show us that masculinity is not to be biologically defined as "being male." And yet, God the Father is ultimately masculine—His

Fatherhood is the fatherhood from which all earthly fatherhood derives its reality (Eph. 3:14–15). We do not call Him "Father" because we have projected our notions of fatherhood up into the heavens. Rather, a dim reflection of His masculinity has been projected, among other places, onto human maleness. So, according to the design of God, when a man marries a woman, he is commanded to enact the masculine role in his relationship with her, and he is equipped by God to do so. This enactment is in line with how God made him. To the extent that he has difficulty doing this, it should be understood as a function of sin and not a function of creaturely limits.

So men are different from women. This ought not to be a shocker, but in these confused times, it still is. We are different because God created us to be able to fulfill the roles He was planning on assigning to us. But the following characteristics are not how men are to be in *every* relationship they may find themselves in. In fact, in some settings, where they are called to be submissive, obedient, grateful, and responsive, they may have to learn to enact a "feminine" role in such a way as to make them much more sympathetic to their wives, seeing as their wives are called to the same thing with regard to them.

For example, when a man lives dutifully as an employee, a subordinate in the military, a church member, or as a son, this can all be used to make men more understanding as they live with their wives (1 Pet. 3:7). It can also be used to show wives that their husbands are not the kind of men who simply utter decrees from on high. They are *in* authority, but also visibly *under* authority, and they know what it is like.

We said earlier that masculinity was to be understood as *authority, sacrifice, responsibility*, and *initiative*. Let us consider these in turn, and remember that we are talking about men in relation to their wives.

Authority. Being masculine involves authority, rule, and the right to make decisions that affect others. But in ruling, and in making decisions, it is paramount that husbands remember what authority is for: "For though I should boast somewhat more of our authority, which the Lord hath *given us for edification*, and not for your destruction, I should not be ashamed" (2 Cor. 10:8). We see the same kind of thing with regard to civil authority: "When the righteous are in authority, the people rejoice: but when the wicked beareth rule, the people mourn" (Prov. 29:2). This is the necessary combination—righteousness, authority, and consequent rejoicing. When this is abused by husbands, wives are tempted to usurp authority, which of course is not becoming (1 Tim. 2:12).

Sacrifice. The masculinity of Christ is clearly set forth in His willingness to lay down His life. Not only did He do this at the climax of His life when He suffered on the cross, but He also did this throughout the course of His perfect sacrificial life (Eph. 5:25). It is impossible to die well without living well. So, in all those incidents over the checkbook, or the garbage, or the misplaced tool, a man is telegraphing his willingness or unwillingness to die for his wife. He is saying, "If I am not willing to sacrifice this small thing for you, how much less would I lay down my life for you?" He may not think he is saying this, but he is. If I won't give you a quarter, why would I give you a million dollars?

Responsibility. Christ did not just die *instead* of His bride, He died *on account of* His bride. Now of course, as stated before, sinful husbands cannot reenact a substitutionary death, but nevertheless all husbands are commanded to imitate a substitutionary death (Eph. 5:27–28). This is the single most difficult thing for selfish husbands to learn. Until the Holy Spirit touches a man's heart, this is not just an insurmountable height to climb (with "climbing" well understood); it is an indecipherable mass of unintelligible symbols. Jumping to the moon is easy to understand but impossible to do. Doing higher levels of calculus is actually possible but (for me at any rate) much more difficult to understand. Telling a sinful, fallen man to accept responsibility for things he didn't do seems like the epitome of crazy talk. He has enough trouble taking responsibility for his own actions. What kind of sense does it make to tell him to take responsibility for things his wife did? And what does it mean to "take responsibility" in this way? The short version is that it means the husband comes before God in prayer and confesses the state of the marriage and family. He confesses as the federal representative of that household. He says, "God, *we* have done this and that." As he learns to do this, he starts to grow in moral authority, because authority flows to those who take responsibility.

Initiative. In a wedding ceremony, the bridegroom does not wait for the bride to come to him—he takes the initiative by going and getting her. Again, this is what Jesus did for us, and this is what real masculinity looks like—it grasps the initiative. Unless it is resting (from the work that follows initiative), sitting around squandering time is a functional denial of masculinity.

Having addressed the question of masculinity and how men are different from women, we now turn, as promised, to *femininity*, and how women are different from men. Please remember that our central concern (at this point) is not raw biology, but rather how the broader questions of masculinity and femininity relate to our obedience as men and women.

> Likewise, ye wives, be in subjection to your own husbands; that, if any obey not the word, they also may without the word be won by the conversation of the wives; While they behold your chaste conversation coupled with fear. Whose adorning let it not be that outward adorning of plaiting the hair, and of wearing of gold, or of putting on of apparel; But let it be the hidden man of the heart, in that which is not corruptible, even the ornament of a meek and quiet spirit, which is in the sight of God of great price. For after this manner in the old time the holy women also, who trusted in God, adorned themselves, being in subjection unto their own husbands: Even as Sara obeyed Abraham, calling him lord: whose daughters ye are, as long as ye do well, and are not afraid with any amazement. (1 Pet. 3:1–6)

Peter begins by telling wives how to respond to disobedient husbands (vv. 1–2): they should try to win their husbands over without a word, through a chaste way of life coupled with reverence. St. Peter tells them not to try to "hold" their husbands by means of outward adornment (v. 3); rather, wives should adorn themselves for God, and they should do it in the way that most pleases God. The contrast here is not between adornment (bad) and non-adornment (good). Rather, the contrast is between superficial adornment that washes off in the sink and true adornment that is of great value in the sight of God (v. 4). This is how the holy women in ancient times did it, trusting in God, adorning themselves, and submitting to their husbands (v. 5). Sarah did this, obeying her husband, calling him lord—this is the basis for liberation from fear (v. 6).

God designed the characteristics of femininity to complement those of masculinity. In the first half of this chapter, we saw that masculinity is authority, sacrifice, responsibility, and initiative. We are now considering the feminine counterpart—femininity is submission, obedience, gratitude, and responsiveness. But it is important for us to remember, each of us, not only what we are doing, but in which direction we are doing it. Women are supposed to be feminine in relation to their own husbands and not in every direction generally. Older women are supposed to teach younger women (Tit. 2:3–4); women are supposed to issue commands to stubborn two-year-old boys (Eph. 6:1); and women are not supposed to obey another woman's husband (Eph. 5:22). Grown men are supposed to remember the law of their mother (Prov. 6:20), and a queen is supposed to guide her husband the king into wisdom (Est. 5:2). All this means that, if false notions of femininity are widely accepted in the Christian community, then the most feminine wives will not necessarily be recognized as such. Femininity is not to be defined as a frilly, frothy giggling. It is hard to imagine Elsie Dinsmore playing the role of Jael, the wife of Heber.

There is a related issue: when a man is "effeminate," we mean he is displaying feminine characteristics in an inappropriate way or in an inappropriate direction. An abdicating man (toward his wife) is being effeminate. An obedient foot soldier charging a hill is appropriately obedient and is not being effeminate. In a similar way, feminists are at war (ironically) with femininity, and they try to adopt a masculine posture in inappropriate ways and directions. Both kinds of sins put everything out of kilter. However sincere you are, and however industrious you may be, it is not possible to thread a nut onto a bolt by turning it counter-clockwise. This is why the best description of abdicators (husbands) and usurpers (wives) is *frustrated*.

So women are different from men. What can we learn about femininity (toward husbands) from the women of old? How does St. Peter apply it?

Submission. Biblically speaking, submission is a demeanor of *adornment*. A craven wife is not a submissive wife. Being cowed is not being submissive. A wife who flinches (inside or out) when her husband speaks is not a submissive wife. What are the pearls on the necklace that God admires (v. 4)? They are chastity, reverence, gentleness and quietness of spirit, subjection to her own husband, obedience, and freedom from fear. The word that comes to mind is *lady*. The world's hatred of the word *submission* is actually the world's hatred of loveliness in wives—the world hates true adornment. Think of submission primarily as a disposition, demeanor, or character trait, and not as though it consisted simply of this action or that one. Submission pervades a marriage; acts of overt obedience might be few and far between.

Obedience. Nevertheless, it says in our text that Sarah obeyed Abraham (v. 6). Obedience is borne of submission and is one focused characteristic of it. Titus 2:5 says that wives are to be taught by the older women to be "obedient to their own husbands." But though obedience to husbands is part of submission, it should not be equated with submission. An "obedient" but surly wife is unsubmissive, and a wife who makes a display of her conservative, traditional-values submissiveness is simply a holdover from the early forms of nineteenth-century feminism. Nevertheless, after all such necessary qualifications are made, the

Christian world still needs a book entitled *Obey Your Husband and Other Novel Ideas*. I can hear an angry mob gathering right now, so I might as well finish the point. No human authority is absolute, and this includes the authority of the husband. But it is real, nonetheless, and most Christian wives who disobey (or disregard) their husbands are not in the category of "obeying God rather than men."

Gratitude. Wives are to learn from the Church how to be wives (Eph. 5:24), and gratitude is one of the central characteristics of the bride of Christ. Christian worship is a *eucharistic* service, a service of thanksgiving. Thanksgiving is therefore at the center of femininity. Moreover, thanksgiving to a husband (who works, provides, protects, and leads) is closely related to respect, which wives are also called to.

Responsiveness. The relation between husband and wife is not static. He does not sit *here,* being masculine, with her over *there,* being feminine. They do not radiate vibes across the room at each other. Their relationship is instead a dynamic exchange. He initiates, and she responds—this glorious dance should pervade every aspect of their lives. He bows, and then she curtsies. We love because He first loved us (1 Jn. 4:19). And we learn to love each other the way He first loved us.

Duties of Husbands and Wives

We have discussed what husbands' orientation and demeanor toward their wives should be (masculinity), but all of this will remain merely theoretical unless we make a point of applying it to ourselves in close imitation of the Incarnation. So what are the specific duties of husbands? We may divide them into two broad categories—*protection* and *provision*.

> And I looked, and rose up, and said unto the nobles, and to the rulers, and to the rest of the people, Be not ye afraid of them: remember the Lord, which is great and terrible, and fight for your brethren, your sons, and your daughters, your wives, and your houses. (Neh. 4:14)

> But if any provide not for his own, and specially for those of his own house, he hath denied the faith, and is worse than an infidel. (1 Tim. 5:8)

These two texts provide us with two examples of husbands and fathers being given their marching orders. Husbands are called by God to protect and provide for their wives and families. The context of the Nehemiah passage is the return of the exiles to Jerusalem, when the enemies of God gathered and threatened them. "But it came to pass, that when Sanballat, and Tobiah, and the Arabians, and the Ammonites, and the Ashdodites, heard that the walls of Jerusalem were made up, and that the breaches began to be stopped, then they were very wroth" (Neh. 4:7). In the second text, the apostle Paul is dealing with the church's various obligations to take care of people and makes it very plain that the first line of provision lies with the family provider, who is the head of that house.

So, one of the fundamental duties that God assigns to husbands is that of protection. But protection from what? The first answer to this question lies at the level of definition. The protector must not be one that the protected needs protection from. If her guardian is corrupt, what is a wife supposed to do? This means that the protector must never himself inflict physical threats or harm, verbal threats or harm, or the pain of treachery and marital infidelity.

Second, the husband must protect his wife from physical harm, from local situations up to national ones. She does not need to believe him to have superhuman powers or to be in any way invincible, but in order for her to be emotionally secure, she needs to know that in any threatening situation, he would be in between her and the threat, and that he would die before she did. This is the meaning of our text from Nehemiah, and it has many very down-to-earth ramifications for how we bring up our boys.

In the third place, a husband must also be vigilant to protect his wife from spiritual harm. This is what Adam failed to do in the garden and what Jesus faithfully did for us. A priest is one who guards and protects the sanctuary, and in this sense every Christian man is a priest in his home: "for I have espoused you to one husband" (2 Cor. 11:1–4). The failure of Adam at this point was his fundamental failure, and it is the point where many of his male descendents find it far too easy to follow his example. This takes us back to our earlier chapter on jealousy. Husbands need to learn how to be jealous for the virtue and reputation of their wives.

But the same question arises when we talk about provision. What is the duty of a godly husband when it comes to provision?

"If he take him another wife; her food, her raiment, and her duty of marriage, shall he not diminish. And if he do not these three unto her, then shall she go out free without money" (Exod. 21:10–11). This law is one of the restraints that God placed on the practice of polygamy during the times of the older covenant. This was no endorsement of polygamy; it was rather one of many restrictions that the law of God placed on the practice in order to lead the people of God into the full Christian conception of monogamous marriage. But with that said, we can still see what a biblical husband is called upon to provide for his wife. If a man cannot withhold any of these three things from his wife upon taking a second wife, how much more shall he not withhold any of them because he "slept in," or "twisted his ankle"? The three things he must provide for her are food, clothing, and conjugal relations. Of course, all of these are not provided by the husband absolutely, as though he were a god, but rather under the sovereignty of God.

Complete cupboards. A man is called by God to provide his wife with the food she needs to do what God has called her to do. He provides, and she manages. Remember that what we are dealing with is prioritization. This is not a command from God to every husband to "be rich." But every household budget has certain non-negotiable items—and the groceries fund should come right after the tithe. He provides for her, in other words, before he spends his own fun money on various recreational "needs." Her grocery money comes before his shotgun shells or pipe tobacco. When a belt needs to be tightened, it needs to be his.

Complete closets. A wife is the adornment of her husband, and therefore it is important for the husband to adorn her. The desire to be adorned is not to be dismissed as mere vanity or frippery. Of course, if it gets out of balance it may become that, but the fact remains that God requires husbands to clothe their wives. And doing this should be a higher priority for him than buying a new outboard motor.

Complete union. This requirement is not just simply sexual in nature; it is also related to the biological purpose of sexual relations, which is the propagation of offspring. We know the Bible well enough to know that there are other purposes for sexual union (communion and prevention of immorality), but this purpose remains. A husband is not just to provide his wife with children (there are fertilization clinics that can do that in an impersonal way), but he is to provide her with children who will grow up with a faithful father.

There is more to this command of provision, however. In Ephesians 5:29, husbands are told to "nourish and cherish" their wives as they do their own bodies. That means that husbands cannot mechanically provide for their wives in some financial way, as though God required nothing more of them than to be an ATM machine. The image of nourishing is an organic one—it is no mere bookkeeping transaction. And the word for *cherish* here literally means "to keep warm." The husband cannot drop the grocery bags on the counter and say, "Here's your stupid food."

The requirement to clothe a wife is literally and practically to be applied, but it also provides us with a metaphor. A man is to protect, guard, keep, and provide for his wife because he is charged by God with the duty of keeping her warm. And that is precisely what the right kind of protection and provision does.

Now just as femininity "answers to" masculinity, so the duties of wives answer to the duties of husbands—it is almost as though God designed us to live together. So now we come to the particular duties of wives. We have to remember the same distinctions we covered when talking about the duties of husbands; that is, we have to remember the difference between *being* and *doing*. Wives must be careful not to rush off to work through a list of do's and don'ts without understanding that it all flows from a demeanor of grace, a gentle and quiet spirit.

The aged women likewise, that they be in behaviour as becometh holiness, not false accusers, not given to much wine, teachers of good things; that they may teach the young women to be sober, to love their husbands, to love their children, to be discreet, chaste, keepers at home, good, obedient to their own husbands, that the word of God be not blasphemed. (Tit. 2:3–5)

It is assumed here that the older women have a long and wise experience with their own husbands and families, and that in personal character they are holy—not false accusers and not given to much wine, for example. Now when the commands of God are given to particular classes of people, we should assume that there is a reason for gearing the instruction that way: it matches up with the temptations of that particular class. Older women are told to be holy in their behavior, and holy means "set apart" or "distinct." They are told not to accuse falsely, and conversely they are also to be zealous for the reputations of others. They are warned away from too much wine. Given this basic character, they are to be teachers of good things.

The particular things that younger wives need to learn from older wives are clearly laid out in the text. The first is *sobriety*, which refers to more than just alcohol. Young women need to be taught moderation and temperance in all things. They need to learn to be "into husbands" and "into kids." The words are *philandros* and *philoteknos* respectively—"husband-lovers" and "kid-lovers" (more on this shortly). They must learn discretion, which is very close to the first lesson of sobriety. They must be chaste, which not only refers to sexual purity but also involves the stirring up of *reverence*. Again, it means to be a lady. They are to learn to be an *oikouros*, which literally means "house-guard." Pay close attention to what that word actually requires: they are to guard the home. They are also to be taught *goodness*, as well as obedience to their own husbands.

This is reciprocity. When a husband is called to do something, it follows from this that his wife is called to be a help to him in doing it. Recall that femininity is *responsive*, not a competing initiation. This means that when a husband is trying to learn how to take his responsibilities seriously, and he doesn't really know how it is all to be done, the wife should offer him genuine help. But what too often happens is that a young husband goes to take some action, his wife challenges him from behind, and he finds himself having to figure out a challenge on two fronts—and one was difficult enough. This principle does not deny the importance of wifely input, but rather insists on wisdom in the timing of it. Examples may be found in all manner of circumstances—disciplining kids, dealing with in-laws, controversy with a neighbor, and so on.

So wives are to be "into husbands" and "into kids." But secularist propaganda works, and often Christians will pick up on some of it and repeat it themselves. Suppose a young man of college age wants to be an engineer, which is a perfectly honorable course of action, and he is asked about his plans at church. He says that he would like to be an engineer, and no one hoots at him. Now suppose a young woman desires to be a homemaker, a wife, and a mother. She had better keep *that* to herself, because the vocation that God created her to love and desire is (in our culture) widely despised. Now of course, there is a way for her to voice this desire that would be bad manners (say, while batting her eyes at a single man who inquired), but there is no disputing that domestic responsibility, which God created women to glory in, is regularly insulted in our day. Married woman are routinely asked, "Do you work, or do you stay at home?" This problem is so pervasive it has to be considered an attempt by a secular culture to shape and mold us to its own image. Christian wives and mothers should not let the world press them into its mold (Rom. 12:1–2), but they should not overreact into a neo-Amish approach either.

So, St. Paul outlines the general shape of the curriculum of what the older women should teach the younger, but from this we can draw out three basic, particular duties.

A pleasant home. A wife is always to remember that she is what makes a home pleasant to be in or not. St. Paul here says that she is to be sober, good, discrete, chaste, obedient, and *into* her husband and kids. Let's call this the "sweetheart principle." The flip side of this is that when this goes wrong, it goes really wrong. No one can make a home as pleasant as a godly woman can, and no one can make a home as unpleasant as an ungodly woman can: "It is better to dwell in the wilderness, than with a contentious and an angry woman" (Prov. 21:19); "A continual dropping in a very rainy day and a contentious woman are alike" (Prov. 27:15). Many men do not work long hours because they are in love with their jobs—it just beats the alternative of having to be at home. And if the choice were between going home and getting a root canal, they might just go for the dentist.

A well-run home. The Bible does not teach that a woman's place is in the home, but it does teach that a godly woman's priority is her home. The balance between the two can be clearly seen in Proverbs 31. Christian women need to live in such a way that the taunt "Do you work?" becomes funny. This means, incidentally, that gadding about and "fellowship" are not to be substituted for the diligent work that the average home needs.

The home as a course of study. The older women are teaching these things, and the younger wives are called to be learning them. This means paying attention to your lessons: study your husband, study your children, study your schedule, and study your virtues and your failings.

It is important for young women to figure this out not just for their own homes, but for their future duty as teachers. The day is coming when they will be the ones teaching the younger women, and they don't want to be in the position of saying, "Oh, I don't know, really. I just sort of muddled through."

Headship

We come now to the question of what headship is and is not. It is not enough for us to *use* the biblical words and phrases; we must know what they *mean* in Scripture.

> Look not every man on his own things, but every man also on the things of others. Let this mind be in you, which was also in Christ Jesus: Who, being in the form of God, thought it not robbery to be equal with God: But made himself of no reputation, and took upon him the form of a servant, and was made in the likeness of men: And being found in fashion as a man, he humbled himself, and became obedient unto death, even the death of the cross. Wherefore God also hath highly exalted him, and given him a name which is above every name: That at the name of Jesus every knee should bow, of things in heaven, and things in earth, and things under the earth; And that every tongue should confess that Jesus Christ is Lord, to the glory of God the Father. (Phil. 2:4–11)

When we consider the three persons of the holy Trinity, we must not fall into the heretical mistake of thinking that, out of the three of them, Jesus is the humble one. Jesus humbled Himself to the point of death, and the magnitude of this humbling is precisely what reveals who He is. Jesus humbles Himself to the Father because this is what reveals the Father. This is what the Father and Holy Spirit are like also in their mutual self-giving.

The salvation that God is working into us is actually God Himself—God gives Himself in our salvation. Not surprisingly, when men refuse to have the character of our triune God worked into them, and instead worship a false god, they become like the idol they worship (Ps. 115). If that idol is a mental construct of God that is not in line with Scripture, then that construct is a non-trinitarian heresy. Interestingly, two of the most common trinitarian heresies line up nicely with two of the most common marital approximations of those heresies.

The heresy of Arianism says that subordination must mean inequality. And since Jesus is clearly submissive to the Father, this must mean that He is not equal to the Father. This must mean that He is "like" the Father, not that He is "equal to" the Father. This is believed because it is simply assumed that submission means inferiority. To make this assumption is to fall into the Arian mistake. Arians make this mistake with regard to the nature of God, and husbands who browbeat their wives make the same mistake with regard to marriage. But the fact that a wife submits to her husband does not mean that she is somehow his inferior—only an Arian would think that.

The heresy of modalism assumes the same kind of thing in an opposite way—that equality must mean that the subordination is only apparent, not real. So it is assumed that there is only one unitary God, and this one God manifests Himself in different ways, using different "masks" to communicate with us. The shared assumption of both heresies is that trying to put submission and equality together is like trying to square the circle. But God reveals Himself to us—in Scripture—as triune. The three equal persons of the Trinity do not fight over glory, and genuine submission occurs within that Trinity. Those who fall into the marital counterparts to these heresies may use the biblical language of headship or equality, but we must firmly reject both errors. This is what headship is not.

The Arian husband starts with subordination—with what he thinks the doctrine of submission means—and then applies it to his world accordingly. Because he knows that his wife is to submit to him ("Ephesians 5!") he concludes falsely that she occupies a lesser plane. He considers her to be his inferior, and whenever he is called up to defend this view he does not turn to passages that teach the woman's inferiority (for there are none), but rather turns to passages that clearly teach the wife's duty to render submission—and there are many of those. But what does a wife render to her husband that Christ did not render to the Father? If submission means inferiority, what does this do to our theology of the holy Trinity?

Another important point to make is that heretics can be either nice or mean. There are despotic husbands in the grip of this error, and they make a living hell for their wives. But the error does not go away just because you put a happy face on it. The heresy remains, and it is still destructive. How would this manifest itself? Through paternalism—condescending references to the "little woman" and patting her on her silly little head. All this may not be malicious or despotic, but it is still wrong.

Then there are the modalist husbands. Feminism (including the evangelical "lite" versions) is a reaction to this kind of marital Arianism, and it lurches into the opposite error. Since men and women are equal, so the thinking goes, there must be no submission at all. There are different mechanisms for getting rid of submission: assuming a unitary god with different faces is one such technique, and turning marriage into a straightforward roommate fifty-fifty situation is another. Such a marriage has no locus of responsibility, and because marriage is a fundamental creation design, the result is that both the husband and wife are exasperated and frustrated—but given their theology on the subject, they don't really know why.

In our text from Philippians, we are told that Jesus humbled Himself before God and that, in doing this, He was like God. We are also told that we are to humble ourselves to one another just as Jesus did. Because we are under His authority, we are therefore to model His humility, and *all* Christians are to do this for one another. That being the case, how much more are husbands and wives to "have this mind which was also in Christ Jesus"? Because a wife is under her husband's authority, she is to model his humility. Because a husband is in authority, he is to use that authority as the basis from which to sacrifice. In doing this, the wife does not lose her equality with her husband; rather, she establishes it. In doing this, the husband does not lose his authority with his wife; rather, he establishes it.

All this said, we still need to take careful pains to understand what headship actually is, so that we might live out this understanding obediently. "For the husband is the head of the wife, even as Christ is the head of the church: and he is the saviour of the body" (Eph. 5:23). Notice in this text that it says that the husband *is* the head of the wife, not that the husband *ought* to be the head of his wife. Obedience and disobedience on the part of a husband does not make him a head or not a head. He is a head regardless, but he can be an obedient head or disobedient head. He can be a head who tells the truth about Christ in his sacrificial love, or he can be a head who lies about Him through selfishness, but silence is not an option. Notice that the husband is the head of the wife in the same way that Christ is the head of His bride, the Church. This means that we may (indeed, we must) learn about our marriages by looking to the ultimate marriage, the final marriage, the last marriage.

Scripture teaches that headship involves "fullness": "And [God] hath put all things under [Christ's] feet, and gave him to be the head over all things to the church, which is his body, the fulness of him that filleth all in all" (Eph. 1:22–23). In Scripture, headship does not mean a stand-alone, autonomous authority. Headship is trinitarian, bestowing fullness from above and summoning fullness from below. The head fills the body, and the head is filled by the body. We have already considered this perichoretic aspect of the universe God made, but we have to recognize that this truth fills all things. By definition, it is not an isolated concept. How could the concept of fullness be separated from that which is filled?

Headship is also sacrificial. This is the import of our text: as soon as the headship of Christ is mentioned over the body, it is immediately added that Christ is the savior of the body (Eph. 5:23). And how did He save the body? He did this by dying on the cross. Likewise, immediately after husbands are told that they are the heads of their wives, the first point of direct application is found in verse 25: *Love as Christ loved.* No man ever hated his own body; the head loves the body, by definition.

Headship is authoritative, but it is a very particular type of authority. Using the prerogatives of an office (any office) in order to accumulate perks is rebellious headship, not obedient headship (Mt. 20:25–26). Godly authority is given to build up, not to tear down (2 Cor. 10:8). Nevertheless, godly authority remains recognizably authoritative, although it must be continually emphasized (in this sinful world) that this is an authority that must have a servant's heart and bleeding hands. There is true authority here (Eph. 5:24), but we must look at the sacrificial context, and as Christians we should see that this is the only context for true authority.

Scripture also teaches us that headship is iconic: "For a man indeed ought not to cover his head, forasmuch as he is the image (*eikon*) and glory of God: but the woman is the glory of the man" (1 Cor. 11:7). We see here a connection between a man's physical head and God (and therefore Christ, his head). We see in this passage a connection between a woman's physical head and her covenant head, her husband. Headship is iconic, which means it is representative. Man and woman are therefore woven together by the ultimate and powerful bonds of metaphor.

So consider the pattern of the headship that Paul weaves here. A woman's head is related to the woman. The woman is related to the man, and so therefore the woman's head is related to the man, her head. The man's head is related to the man, and the man is related to Christ. The man's head is therefore related to Christ. And Christ Himself has a head, who is God the Father. Christ is the *eikon* of the Father, man is *eikon* of Christ, and woman is *eikon* of man. This relates powerfully to the second commandment—in a world full of God-given images, we don't *need* to make any more.

Headship is hierarchical. Headship ascends to the ultimate place, and through the sacrifice of Christ, we see that headship stoops to the lowest place. The one thing it does not do is level everything: "But I would have you know, that the head of every man is Christ; and the head of the woman is the man; and the head of Christ is God" (1 Cor. 11:3). In the world made by our triune God, both exaltation and humility are possible, and they go together. The one thing excluded is a dull, androgynous flatness.

Lastly, headship is covenantal. The apostle Paul teaches us that Adam was a type of the one who was to come, that is, Christ (Rom. 5:14). This idea of headship is right at the center of all this. Just as Adam lost his bride through his disobedience at a tree (along with all her children), so the last Adam won His bride through His obedience at a tree (and that redemption included all the barren woman's children). Through unbelief, Eve became barren, and through faith, Sarah, the barren woman, gave birth to a new world, a new humanity. God offers us covenantal blessing, and we are to receive the blessing of this everlasting covenant by faith.

> Now the God of peace, that brought again from the dead our Lord Jesus, that great shepherd of the sheep, through the blood of the everlasting covenant, make you perfect in every good work to do his will, working in you that which is wellpleasing in his sight, through Jesus Christ; to whom be glory for ever and ever. Amen. (Heb. 13:20–21)

The New Covenant is everlasting, and it will be eternally new when everything sinful has long since passed away. Not only is this the case, but the New Covenant was operative for believers even during the times of the Old Covenant (Heb. 9:15). As we are being knit together with the Head, our Lord Jesus, we have to remember that we are bone of His bone, flesh of His flesh. His blood is for us, and for that reason we are saved. For that reason, we are to live in our marriages as though we were saved in this way.

CHAPTER

10

Submission

Having considered what headship is not, and then what it truly is according to Scripture, we now need to do the same with its complement, submission. In this fallen world, glorious things are slandered and caricatured first, and sometimes the defenders of such things find themselves defending the caricature and not the reality. So if we want to talk about submission at all (much less practice it), we have to begin by rejecting various errors about it.

> And they said unto him, Where is Sarah thy wife? And he said, Behold, in the tent. And he said, I will certainly return unto thee according to the time of life; and, lo, Sarah thy wife shall have a son. And Sarah heard it in the tent door, which was behind him. Now Abraham and Sarah were old and well stricken in age; and it ceased to be with Sarah after the manner of women. Therefore Sarah laughed within herself, saying, After I am waxed old shall I have pleasure, my lord being old also? And the LORD said unto Abraham, Wherefore did Sarah laugh, saying, Shall I of a surety bear a child, which am old? Is any thing too hard for the LORD? At the time appointed I will return unto thee, according to the time of life, and Sarah shall have a son. Then Sarah denied, saying, I laughed not; for she was afraid. And he said, Nay; but thou didst laugh." (Gen. 18:9–15)

There are a number of things we could draw from this passage, but we will limit ourselves to what the apostle Peter takes from it. Peter says that Sarah was one of the holy women of old, in submission to her own husband (1 Pet. 3:5–6). The apostle tells us that Sarah called her husband "lord," but we should note that she was not being obsequious here or flattering—she called him lord in passing and to *herself*. Peter goes on to say that if Christian women do well and imitate Sarah, they will not be afraid with any amazement. It is interesting to note that in this passage, Sarah was afraid and denied having laughed at the incredible promise, but the Lord answered her, and said, "No, but you did laugh." We see later that Sarah conquered her fear (by faith), and she owned her laughter: "And Sarah said, God hath made me to laugh, so that all that hear will laugh with me" (Gen. 21:6). The name Isaac itself means "he laughs." It was a bumpy start, but Sarah conceived Isaac through faith: "Through faith also Sara herself received strength to conceive seed, and was delivered of a child when she was past age, because she judged him faithful who had promised" (Heb. 11:11).

Given the way that God has made the world, submission for women is not optional. They will be submissive in some way and to somebody. Just as we have seen that obedience or disobedience does not make headship go away, neither does obedience or disobedience make submission go away. Disobedience to the word of God means that submission is rendered with a bad grace, with a surly or quarrelsome disposition, or that it is rendered to the wrong men or the wrong entities. But such disobedience does not make the reality disappear.

It is remarkable how many places in Scripture emphasize that women are to be submissive to their *own* husbands. What this means is liberation from having to submit to all the others. Conversely, if a young daughter leaves home because she does not want to submit to her father, she will soon be submitting to others, elsewhere, who do not have her interests at heart. If a woman does not turn to her husband for protection (from sexual harassment, say), she will be turning to (and submitting to) some federal agency—a substitute husband (or father). Submission is inescapable: it is not a matter of whether a woman will be submissive, but rather to which men or entities she will be submissive.

Submission is not academic. In a godly marriage, authority and submission ought not to be constantly noticed, but like the air around us, it is still important to have it around. Scripture addresses this subject constantly, and so we have to take care to get it straight in our minds and hearts. Once it is straight, we can move on to not noticing it. In our circles, we identify ourselves as conservative, evangelical, and Reformed. We have to guard against the temptation of thinking that just because we can say the word submission without blushing that this somehow means we live it. We must guard against the hypocritical self-deception that James warns against (Jas. 1:22). The conservative Christian world has no small number of big-time submission mamas who are anything but submissive.

At the same time, submission is not craven or slavish. Just as men submit to a Christ who showed them how to submit, so women are to submit to Christian husbands who show them how to submit. When this is the way it is done, human submission follows the divine pattern, and the one who humbles himself or herself will be lifted up. A browbeaten wife is not a submissive wife—biblically speaking, submission should bring to mind the concept of a very great and gracious lady. When a woman's crown is placed at a man's feet, the first thing he does is take it and place it on his head (Prov. 12:4).

Submission is not silent. The pattern given to women in submission is the pattern of the Church to Christ, and what does Christ require of His bride? He wants to *hear* from her: "Be careful for nothing; but in every thing by prayer and supplication with thanksgiving let your requests be made known unto God" (Phil. 4:6).

Submission is not a bad testimony; it is quite the reverse. More than once, the apostles link a right relationship of a wife to her husband to a good testimony before pagans. He does not say that this is the case in the first century only—that is, that such is a good testimony in a Greco-Roman setting: "that they may teach the young women to be sober, to love their husbands, to love their children, to be discreet, chaste, keepers at home, good, obedient to their own husbands, that the word of God be not blasphemed" (Tit. 2:4–5).

Furthermore, submission is not unitarian. We have emphasized this before, but we have to keep reminding ourselves lest we slip back into understanding submission as an attempt to cope with raw power. That is not it at all. Authority and submission together are a dance, not a fistfight. Moreover, it is a dance grounded in the way things ultimately are, because this is the way our triune God ultimately is. The nature and majesty of God is clearly displayed through the things that are made (Rom. 1:20), and one of the great things made—one of the great mysteries—is the way of a man with a maiden (Prov. 30:19).

So what is submission, then? We have been careful to avoid distortions of this teaching because in our generation it is both embraced and rejected wrongly. Let us look back to 1 Corinthians again for guidance: "For a man indeed ought not to cover his head, forasmuch as he is the image and glory of God: but the woman is the glory of the man" (1 Cor. 11:7). Although this is not a definition in the modern dictionary sense, it is still a definition. Notice what we learn: the woman is the *glory* of the man. The apostle Paul is choosing his language very carefully here. He says that man is the image and glory of God, but he does not say that woman is the image and glory of man. This is because Genesis is very clear that man and woman *together* constitute the image of God: "So God created man in his own image, in the image of God created he him; male and female created he them" (Gen. 1:27). It would be a grievous error even to hint that women were not fashioned in the image of God just as the men are. But star differs from star in glory (1 Cor. 15:40–41), and the glory of the sun and moon are not the same. Glory both ascends and descends—and that is its glory. Glory bows and glory curtsies. Glory shines and glory reflects. Glory empties and glory fills. Glory ascends in the

Shekinah column, and glory descended into the virgin's womb. Glory is anything but domesticated or predictable.

So we return to the idea of a dance. Just a moment ago, the relation of authority and submission was compared to a dance, not a fistfight. It is not a competition. No gentleman bows to a lady after a beautiful dance together and says, "Beat you!" Although the man leads in the dance, the result of his leading is to showcase his lady. This is because he is dancing with his glory, and the last thing in the world he should want to do is upstage his own glory. It would make no sense: "Stop looking at my glory! Look at *me*." If a man were to succeed in getting people to look away from his glory, and look at him instead, the only thing that the observers would wonder is what she was doing with a man like him in the first place.

Submission is growth and maturation into glory. We have seen that the Scriptures teach women in multiple places that they are to be submissive to their own husbands. As forgiven sinners, they are being taught to reassume the position that their mother Eve forfeited through being deceived, and which their father Adam lost for them through his rebellion against the word of God. Before the Fall, certain motions between husband and wife were just natural, normal, right, and effortless. After the Crash (as we might just as well call it), all of us who are redeemed in Christ are going through intensive "physical therapy" in order to relearn some of these fundamental motions. Just like a victim of an automobile accident who has to learn how to use a spoon again, so men have to learn how to take responsibility and women have to learn how to submit. And it can be exasperating to have to be told the same thing by your therapist ten times in a day—exasperating but worth it.

We should not become so consumed with the details of the therapy that we forget the point, which is restoration of the former glory. Submission (rightly understood) is this motion of feminine response to a masculine husband. And what is the wife to that husband? She is his glory. So learning how to respond to him is growing up into glory. If a woman is a man's glory, learning to respond as a woman to a godly man is learning to be glorious.

There are three aspects to this glory. In the passage that follows our text, the apostle Paul gives us three characteristics of women that help us understand what this glory involves. The first is that woman is "from the man" (1 Cor. 11:8). She is his glory because God created Eve from Adam's side (Gen. 2:21). The second is that she was created "for the man" (1 Cor. 11:9). This depends on Gen. 2:18, which says that God created a helper for man that was suitable for him. Third, woman is the glory of man because every man with a wife is a man with a mother (1 Cor. 11:11–12). So glory involves being "from the man," "for the man," and "the mother of men."

First, part of her glory is that she is from the man. In the Scriptures, origins are always important. The fact that woman *was* after the man (and from the man) is the reason why *today* we are not to have women who are elders or pastors (1 Tim. 2:12–13). The origin of woman is not some tidbit of ancient history, nor is it an irrelevant detail: it is a design feature with continuing relevance down to the present day. The God who created the human race in that way continues His work in how He has fashioned every man and woman alive today. This means that a woman who embraces her derivative glory in this is embracing wisdom.

The second point is also important: her glory is being for the man. Two basic questions are these: Where did I come from? Where am I going? The fact that woman is from the man answers the first, and the fact that she was created "for the man" answers the second. Notice (not that I have to tell you to) that this kind of organic interdependency is mortally offensive to the autonomous, individualistic, and atomized spirit of our contemporary age. This spirit wants husbands and wives to be independently functioning roommates. But what should a woman's orientation be? Toward her husband—she was created to be his helper. Notice, though, that when a woman is oriented this way, she is her husband's glory, and not her husband's drudge.

Finally, part of her glory is that she is the mother of men. The apostle Paul knew the sinful heart of men, and he knew that the first two things mentioned here could easily be twisted by men into a vainglorious way of disparaging women. Men are not autonomous any more than women are (1 Cor. 11:11–12). If it is important that the first woman came from the first man, it is also important (obviously) that every man since, from Cain on down, has been born of a woman. To anchor the point for all time, our Lord Jesus was born of a woman.

This is the way God designed us: a woman's derivation is her glory, her task is her glory, and her fertility is her glory. Remember always that distinction and mutual indwelling are trinitarian realities, while independence and autonomy are trinitarian heresies. Denying origins and refusing assigned tasks are trinitarian heresies as well, but receiving what God gave, the way God gave it, is godly gratitude to the triune God who made us all.

CHAPTER

11

Men Are Stupid; So Are Women

The theme of this chapter has been implicit in what has been addressed thus far, but there is still a need to make it explicit. We have to develop the truth that men are stupid, and immediately afterwards, in a completely even-handed way, consider the corresponding truth that women are stupid. A more biblical way of putting this would be to use the term *folly,* which in Scripture is always a question of the heart, and not of the IQ. We are not talking about being dumb, although it might seem that way sometimes; rather, we are talking about what spiritual obtuseness will do to your marriage.

> Likewise, ye husbands, dwell with them according to knowledge, giving honour unto the wife, as unto the weaker vessel, and as being heirs together of the grace of life; that your prayers be not hindered. (1 Pet. 3:7)

The text is just one verse from 1 Peter, but the real text for us to consider is really just three words from that verse—two words in the Greek. Those two words are *kata gnosis,* "according to knowledge." Husbands are called in this verse to dwell with their wives according to knowledge. The results of such knowledge will be the rendering of honor to her, as to a weaker vessel, and treating her as a joint heir of the grace of life. The end result of that wisdom will be that a man's prayers will be not be hindered. So the upshot of this chapter will be to show what *kata gnosis* does not look like. When men are stupid—when they ignore the wisdom of this passage—what kind of mistakes do they make?

Blaming is not leadership. When a man is displeased with something in the home, and lets that displeasure be known, this is not the same thing as leadership. Rightly understood, blaming others is really a confession of a lack of leadership. Being willing to express dissatisfaction is not necessarily a strength. If such expressions are routine, then it is certainly not a strength, but rather a glaring weakness. Many men think that they are being forthright and decisive when they are really just difficult to live with. Leadership involves the assumption of responsibility, not the parceling out of responsibility to others. When a husband speaks, it is life . . . or death. "Death and life are in the power of the tongue: and they that love it shall eat the fruit thereof" (Prov. 18:21). He ought not to assume that simply because he is speaking, it must therefore be a blessing.

Silence is not necessarily agreement. Men often assume that if it has not been spoken to them out loud or written to them in big, block letters, then they must have no responsibility to know it. "Why didn't you tell me?" is sometimes a reasonable question, but far too often it is a dodge and not a real question—the answer might range from "I did, and after twenty times I gave up" to "I was afraid of your response . . . for good reason." The fact that your wife has not expressed disagreement does not mean she agrees. "Counsel in the heart of man is like deep water; but a man of understanding will draw it out" (Prov. 20:5). Men need to learn to actively draw out counsel from their wives.

Laziness is not sexy. Scripture teaches that lust is fundamentally a kind of laziness. Not surprisingly, it is frequently connected to other forms of laziness as well. The more lethargic and unmotivated a man is, the more likely it is that he will think his needs are not being met. "The desire of the slothful killeth him; for his hands refuse to labour. He coveteth greedily all the day long: but the righteous giveth and spareth not" (Prov. 21:25–16).

Laziness knows how to want. The next point is closely related to this one.

Sex is not what many men think. The central problem with pornography is not the immodesty it displays, but rather the lies it tells: "For the lips of a strange woman drop as an honeycomb, and her mouth is smoother than oil" (Prov. 5:3). This is the same woman who can give you, as countless rock songs have promised, a good time "all night long." She is also a flattering liar. In the long run, what she gets you to believe can be far more damaging than what she might be able to get you to do. Often it is Christian men who fall most in this respect—they believe enough of the lie to import discontent into their marriages, but not enough of it to be physically unfaithful.

Brittle pride is not masculine. The male ego is, I am afraid, famous. I have long felt that a pastor has no better diagnostic test for how his congregation is doing spiritually than to arrange a co-ed volleyball game and just watch. Does a man think that it is his responsibility to play every position? How does he handle his mistakes, or those of his teammates? How does he handle defeat and victory? "A man shall be commended according to his wisdom: but he that is of a perverse heart shall be despised" (Prov. 12:8). When the male ego is on a rampage, the only thing to do is stare in disbelief.

Helping is not effeminate. If a man's masculinity washes off in dishwater, then it was a pretty superficial masculinity. If a man does not know how to be a help around the home, instead of being a lump on the couch, then he has a thin view of his own calling. "There is that scattereth, and yet increaseth; and there is that withholdeth more than is meet, but it tendeth to poverty. The liberal soul shall be made fat: and he that watereth shall be watered also himself" (Prov. 11:24–25). What is true in the world generally is true in the home specifically. Men who are helpful to their wives are men who understand they are helping to make their home a blessed place.

Material provision is not a substitute for the provider. A very common mistake that men make is that of substituting their income and their provision for themselves—for their presence and active involvement in the family. Of course men should work hard, and of course they should provide. But the provision must be a token of all the rest of their responsibilities, not a substitute for them. "He that trusteth in his riches shall fall: but the righteous shall flourish as a branch" (Prov. 11:28).

Marriage rests on grace. Remember that living together with your wife is an expression of gospel, not law. You are living together with her with wisdom and understanding, which is why you see that both of you are heirs together of the grace of life. But lack of wisdom does not see the gospel here because folly cannot see the gospel anywhere. The way we live reflects whether or not we know that God has been gracious to us in Christ. We live by grace or we live by works. We live by grace married or we live by works married. If the former, the result is gratitude for the ongoing kindness of God. If the latter, then the result is always some form of misery and condemnation. And in condemning the folly, it is crucial to note that we are not simply being "negative." The only thing we seek to put to death is the way of death.

So we have seen several ways in which men can be morally and spiritually obtuse, but women can be stupid in this sense as well. Men and women are a fallen race together, and women also stumble in their calling to be feminine. Moreover, Christian women, just like Christian men, often call their sins by biblical and spiritual-sounding names.

The 1 Peter passage we considered emphasizes that men need to learn how to live with their wives according to knowledge. In a corresponding way, women have to be taught how to live with their husbands:

> That they may teach the young women to be sober, to love their husbands, to love their children, to be discreet, chaste, keepers

at home, good, obedient to their own husbands, that the word
of God be not blasphemed. (Tit. 2:4–5)

Christian discipleship extends into every area—including the
areas of being a husband or a wife. Young Christian women should
learn diligently from older and wiser Christian women, and St.
Paul here gives us the basic curriculum. First, the young women
need to learn three basic moral attitudes: how to be sober, discrete, and good. Next, they need to learn their orientation within
their basic relationships, by learning how to be husband-lovers,
children-lovers, efficient homemakers, and obedient to their own
husbands. In other words, there is more here than just a simple
requirement—there are multiple lessons to be learned. So in what
ways do women frequently miss what they need to learn? In what
ways can women be stupid in the moral and spiritual sense?

Being unprepared for real leadership. Many a wife desper-
ately wants her husband to be a "spiritual leader," but only to
the extent that he leads where she thinks he should be going.
But if man and wife agree, submission is really a non-issue. If
you think that your husband is making the wrong decision, or is
not acting when he should be acting, that is really the only time
that submission (or obedience) could ever become an issue. As
we have seen from Genesis, part of the curse for the woman was
the desire to master her husband (Gen. 3:16). But in Christian
circles, how would such a desire manifest itself? The husband has
to be critiqued in very "spiritual" terms. "He is not very much of
a spiritual leader. I would be submissive if he would start leading
right." And the whole thing can be couched as a prayer request to
a number of sympathetic friends who are in the same boat.

Trying to lead the leader. This problem can manifest itself
in strange ways and can explain some puzzling behavior. For
example, many women push their husbands to make a decision,
and then they push some more. After pushing a little more after
that, the husband finally—in an "all right, all right" kind of
way—makes a decision to go in that direction. The wife knows

that he is only doing this because she pestered him a great deal, but she still wants him to have made this right decision out of the depths of his own heart. So, in order to give him the opportunity to really mean it now, she begins resisting his implementation of whatever it was. This is the point where he just looks at her without the slightest trace of comprehension. But pushing left and then right is not submission.

Pushing in general is not smart. Many wives push and push, and nothing ever happens. This is because the husband knows he is not much of a spiritual leader—if he were, he would be able to get her to knock that off—but he is enough of a man, he says to himself, "not to be led into leadership by a woman." So he just sits there, defining his masculinity in negative terms: "At least I didn't go along with *that*." In the meantime, she pushes for fifteen years, nothing ever happens, and she concludes that *he* is stupid.

Substituting love for respect. Love and respect are not the same thing. The Bible tells men to love their wives, and wives to respect their husbands. While all human beings should love and respect other human beings, regardless of sex, when it comes to husbands as husbands and wives as wives, the Bible breaks out our fundamental duties. The wives are specifically called to respect their husbands. So while love includes acceptance, security, commitment, and sacrifice, respect involves honor, admiration, and deference. This respect should be directed toward abilities and achievements. Wives who are in a troubled situation should not try to fix it by giving to their husbands only what they as women would like to be receiving (that is, love), because their husbands need respect foremost. Not only is it not going to work, it is not what God said to do.

Emotional pornography. Many women have a problem with pornography, but the use of the word *pornography* here is just a metaphor: pornography is to men what this temptation is to women. What would that temptation be? There are several candidates. The first is found in the tenth commandment: many women need to be aware that they are in as much danger of violating the tenth commandment when they get their Pottery Barn catalog as their husband would be with a copy of the *Sports Illustrated* swimsuit issue. Oftentimes, this temptation to covetousness lets the wife drift into the position where she "hands her husband the apple," urging him to make more money, ask for a raise, and so on; or, through foolish debt, she creates a situation where he is compelled to do that kind of thing.

But another use of pornography is less of a metaphor. In just the way lust is artificially provoked (and inadequately satisfied) through pornography, so a woman's emotions can be artificially stirred (and inadequately satisfied) by a steady diet of sappy romance novels or sappier chick flicks. Just as a man can be tempted to mental unfaithfulness by a pornographic image, so a wife can be tempted to emotional infidelity by over-the-top sentimentalism. This sin, when indulged, introduces additional discontent into the marriage.

In St. Paul's comments, notice the important role that the older women and younger women have. Through their diligent care in how they relate to their husbands, they have the power to protect the gospel against slander, but if they neglect their responsibilities in this, then they open the word of God up to slander. This is why an emphasis on marriage, and responsibilities in marriage, is not a distraction away from the "central things." Marriage is where we live out the central things.

CHAPTER 12

Exchanged Authority

Husbands are to learn the relationship between *love, sacrifice,* and *authority.* In the same way wives are to learn *respect, submission,* and *authority.* In learning these lessons, we are learning what our triune God is like. The element the two sets have in common is obviously that word *authority,* and once we refresh ourselves with the principle, we need to work with some of the nuts and bolts applications.

> And when the ten heard it, they began to be much displeased with James and John. But Jesus called them to him, and saith unto them, Ye know that they which are accounted to rule over the Gentiles exercise lordship over them; and their great ones exercise authority upon them. But so shall it not be among you: but whosoever will be great among you, shall be your minister: And whosoever of you will be the chiefest, shall be servant of all. For even the Son of man came not to be ministered unto, but to minister, and to give his life a ransom for many. (Mk. 10:41–45)

We have already touched on the difference between "right-handed" and "left-handed" authority (to use Martin Luther's phrases). Right-handed authority is straight-line force, while left-handed authority works through indirection—the authority is not obvious. In this passage, Jesus sets the principle before us plainly: the unbelievers view what they call mature authority one way, but Christians are commanded to view it in another way ("But so shall it not be among you").

The problem is not that right-handed, straight-line authority is evil—it is most necessary for Congress, judges, soldiers, policemen, and parents teaching toddlers. But it is not the most *mature* expression of authority, and to believe that it is the only kind of authority for both mature and immature means that one is a totalitarian. Maturity requires that we grow up into the kind of authority that gives itself away. Jesus did this, and He summoned all his followers to do this as well. This means that husbands who want to function as the respected leader in their homes, who want to be "great" among their families, need to come to Jesus Christ in order to die. Do you, as a husband, receive your authority by demanding? Or by bestowing?

This is an issue that must be resolved in the heart first. This is because many times you cannot tell which kind of authority is being exercised by simply recording the action that it takes. One man might require his six-year-old boy to say "Thank you" because the father was irritated by the boy's ingratitude; another man might require it because he wants to bestow the habit of good manners on his boy, so that his son will be blessed throughout the course of his life. The two fathers are in one sense doing exactly the same thing (making their sons say "Thank you"), but in another sense they are doing radically different things (*taking* versus *bestowing*).

In marriage, a man who requires something of his wife might be making the biggest sacrifice of his life. Or he might be acting like a dope. Settle these things in your heart before the Lord. Once a man has come to Jesus in order to be put to death, he may then (after the fact) do as he pleases. But unless he has died, nothing he does (however technically correct) will be right.

So let us assume that a man has this peculiar kind of "left-handed" authority. What is he to do with it? What are some test cases? Incarnational living always comes down to the particulars; abstractions are gloriously true and never make anyone mad. The illustrations that follow are just that—illustrations—and are not meant to be exhaustive. But faithful living means getting down into the details.

We have already addressed the husband's responsibility to provide for his household. The man of the house is certainly called to provide his wife with the wherewithal to discharge her responsibilities, but the wife has a corresponding responsibility to do him good, not harm, all the days of his life. So, buying a truckload of stuff is not necessarily "saving money" because it was all 20 percent off. That may well be, but the remaining 80 percent is still much more than what they want or need. Godly wives are self-governed in this, but that is a subject for another time. My point here is that a man ought not to think that he can discharge all his responsibilities in this area by simply working harder, getting a raise, or a second job—and saying nothing to his wife. That might float the financial boat, but it might also indicate some real problems that cannot be solved unless he can lead her into financial responsibility. The basic question is this: Can a man and his wife have an intelligent discussion about the checkbook without conflict? Has he put enough sacrifice in *his* "leadership checkbook" to write *that* particular check?

There is also the question of the in-laws. Genesis tells us that a man leaves his father and mother and cleaves to his wife, while the parents of the bride give her in marriage. Putting these two things together, we see that a new household unit is created. Certain obligations to the in-laws remain, but the entire picture changes. Children must honor father and mother throughout their lives, and not just while they are home and under parental authority, but the form of this honor changes. The issues that most frequently need to be worked out are *time* and *lines of authority:* How much time do you spend with each set of in-laws? And how can you clarify their roles regarding your own children, particularly with regard to discipline? The better you do with the first, the more difficulty you will have with the latter, and the better you do with the latter, the more difficulty you will have with the former. If the grandparents spend a lot of time around the grand-kids, it is possible that they (and the kids) start thinking of them in a parental role, and lines of authority can get confused. But if lines of authority are enforced with an iron strictness, it might become difficult to spend much time together. However, if the in-laws are walking with the Lord and understand the principles involved, they can be a great help in working out the boundaries on this. A husband needs to assume the responsibility of decid-ing how much time will be spent with the families on each side, and as well as the responsibility of determining how discipline and instruction will be handled when his children are around the extended family. And in doing this, it is not unlikely that he will discover the meaning of sacrifice.

This is not a book on rearing children, but children do come into marriages, and their presence certainly affects those mar-riages. One of the most common areas of trouble in a marriage has to do with the education and discipline of the kids. Two sample problems are dad's tendency to be detached from nurture and education, and the differences between mom and dad's dis-cipline styles.

Delegation is not the same thing as capitulation or surrender. A husband who visits regularly with his wife about how discipline or home schooling is going, or how the kids are doing spiritually, is a delegating father. But if he does not, then he is an abdicating father—and an abdicating father is one who is leaving his wife in the lurch.

One of the best ways for a man to love a woman is to love her children. This means caring enough to be involved and to know what is going on. When was the last time you spent one-on-one time with each of your kids? Do your kids have blogs? How come? If they do, do you read them? Finally, recognize that your children's loyalty to you and your wife will almost certainly be a function of your loyalty to them, and your loyalty to them is also a ministry to your wife.

So now we have to consider the wife's responsibility in all of this. We mentioned earlier that her role consists of *respect, submission*, and *authority*. We have looked at love, sacrifice, and authority with regard to husbands, and now we need to consider the other side of the coin. Remember that authority in the Christian framework is trinitarian authority, in which authority gladly surrendered is the foundation of authority bestowed. This is true of husbands and wives both, though in different ways.

> Wisdom hath builded her house, she hath hewn out her seven pillars: she has killed her beasts; she hath mingled her wine; she hath also furnished her table. She hath sent forth her maidens: she crieth upon the highest places of the city, whoso is simple, let him turn in hither: as for him that wanteth understanding, she saith to him, Come, eat of my bread, and drink of the wine which I have mingled. Forsake the foolish, and live; and go in the way of understanding. (Prov. 9:1–6)

Before looking at this particular text, we need to take a step back and consider that in the book of Proverbs, *wisdom is a woman*. And lest we rush to conclusions, recall that folly is also a woman. The point is that men are summoned to court wisdom and to avoid being seduced by folly. The language of the passage describes wisdom as a great lady who has prepared a great banquet. She has built her house, she has overseen the slaughter of the cattle, she has mixed the wine, and she has set the table. She directs her servant girls, and sends out invitations, calling her guests to come and learn wisdom. Those who are simple and those who are lacking understanding are invited to come. They are told to come eat her bread and drink her wine. In doing this, they forsake foolishness (which is another kind of woman) and learn to live in the way of understanding.

In this world, wisdom is not just found lying on the ground. Wisdom is not something that women *automatically* possess or represent to others. Given the structure of the world, they must automatically represent wisdom *or* folly. They must be a particular embodiment of one or the other.

Take the image that is found in this text. When wisdom builds the house of seven pillars, when she tells one of the men servants to slaughter the cattle, when she selects her wines, when she is busy with the seating arrangements, when she decorates the table, and when she addresses the invitations, what kind of picture do we have? We see a woman who is a great lady, one with authority (over the stables, the wine cellar, the servants' quarters, the kitchen), and that authority is all expended in service to others. In short, we have a hostess. This is the model—the ultimate in feminine service does not cause us to walk into the house, point at the hostess, and say, "Who's the drudge?" When wisdom serves in this way, her authority rises and grows. This is the case even when, as here, she is giving her invitations to simpletons and buffoons.

By its egalitarianism, our culture has declared war on the true authority of the Christian woman. The movement's strategy has been twofold, using both taunts and lies. A woman's grace and authority (consistent with true biblical femininity) consist in her being a lady, and the taunts are predictable—"church ladies," meaning censorious old biddies, are dismissed as being fussy, prissy busybodies. The idea of wisdom, stature, and glory do not enter the picture at all. Of course, it doesn't help when certain women help fulfill the caricature by actually becoming censorious old biddies, but that is beside the point. Moreover, by emphasizing that a Christian woman should aspire to be a lady, it is important that we do not confound this ideal of Christian womanhood with the idea of being rich. Conducting yourself with grace and dignity is not expensive.

Many lies are directed against younger women today—they are told, for example, that true fulfillment will come in the corporate world (in which women are constantly exhorted to try to become like men). Another lie—related to the first in that it denies femininity—falls under the heading of what we might call "lowlife authenticity." For about three centuries, we have been taught (by the devil, or someone very much like him) that grime is more "authentic" than being clean, being disheveled is more real than being put together, and so on. Like most lies of this nature, the destructive impact of it falls most heavily on women. When a woman's authority consists of learning to act like a lady, what happens when the idea of being a lady, or "acting like a lady," is hooted off the public stage? The answer is that young women, shut out from their natural femininity, are left with no good options. Because of our culture-wide "mandatory slovenliness," many young women have been robbed of their glory.

So we must take care not to fall into an anti-feminine egalitarianism, but we must do so by understanding and honoring true feminine authority. Lady wisdom has a house with seven pillars, an image which gloriously conveys such authority. While we are here, we should also note that egalitarianism seeks to strip women of their authority because egalitarianism is against all God-given authority. But the Bible never teaches that it is wrong to strive to obtain the authority that God has granted to you. The issue is always how we properly use that authority. Jesus does not say that we are to rip out the chief seats in the synagogue, but rather how to relate to them. He does not teach us to get rid of seats of honor at banquets—He teaches us how to get *into* them. He does not say that it is wrong to want to be great in the kingdom of heaven; He shows us how to become great in the kingdom of heaven. The glorious thing is that His method of doing this (becoming the servant of all) is a great way of removing the toxins of selfishness that will almost certainly be corrupting our ambition. This said, a Christian woman ought to want to bear and represent godly authority in her home. How should this be done?

When a woman serves in the way described in our text, she is serving in a way that increases her stature in the household, as well as in the mind and heart of her husband. But in order to for this to "work," the service must be seen as a sacrifice offered to God and not a trick offered to her husband. If a woman says, "If I do this, my husband will be maneuvered into thinking that I am really something," this is all wrong. But if she says that this is how God describes Wisdom (the lady) in Scripture, that she wants to imitate it, and that she wants to embody the same kind of thing in her own life, God blesses will bless her efforts.

If Lady Wisdom (with all her wisdom) from the book of Proverbs were placed into your situation, how would she prepare dinner tonight? How would she mix the wine? How would she decorate the dining room? The living room? How would she make love? How would direct the work of the children? How would she carry herself? How would she dress?

The Christian faith does not take authority away from women at all. In fact, it is the only way that women in this world have ever really had any true authority at all. And the words of our Lord Jesus are fulfilled. The first will be last, and the last first.

PART III:
Marriage is for Sinners

13

Lies About Equality

In looking at the differences between masculine and feminine, and in considering the respective duties of husbands and wives, we have been assuming that differences between the sexes exist. But what are those differences, and how can they be understood together with what the Scriptures teach us about our equality in Christ? For anyone involved in the debates about feminism and egalitarianism in the Church, the text is a familiar one.

> For as many of you as have been baptized into Christ have put on Christ. There is neither Jew nor Greek, there is neither bond nor free, there is neither male nor female: for ye are all one in Christ Jesus. And if ye be Christ's, then are ye Abraham's seed, and heirs according to the promise. (Gal. 3:27–29)

For those familiar with everything St. Paul wrote, nothing is clearer than the fact that the apostle affirms and reinforces various social distinctions and hierarchies. Some of them are the result of the Fall (that is, not in the created order of things), like the master/slave relation, but they are still taken at face value in some way (1 Tim. 6:1–5). The meaning of the gospel is applied to such relations with the full expectation that reformation will occur over time. Other social distinctions, like the distinction between Jew and Gentile, are the result of the history of redemption (Rom. 2:9–10), and still others are grounded in the creation order (1 Tim. 2:13–15). But in the passage quoted above, St.

Paul takes on all three and says that unity in Christ Jesus means that such distinctions amount to nothing—but in what respect do they amount to "nothing"? The context makes it plain that anyone from any of these categories (Jew and Gentile, bond and free, male and female) can "put on Christ," can be "one in Christ Jesus," can be "Abraham's seed," and can be inheritors of "the promise." In short, the gospel of Christ is for all.

The Christian faith teaches and brings true biblical equality. The Christian faith also rejects egalitarianism, which is a false definition of equality. Christian equality can be described as *equity*, or even-handedness. Egalitarianism, in contrast, demands sameness, or equality of outcome. These two visions of equality are about as comparable as dry and wet. Think of it in terms of ten teenage boys trying to dunk a basketball: equity means that they all face the same ten-foot standard, and only two of them can do it—equity thus usually means differences in outcome. Egalitarianism wants equality of outcome, and there is only one way to get that—lower the net. Sameness of outcome requires differences in the standards.

The Bible requires a godly equity—we are all offered the same law and the same gospel. The standard is always grounded on our immutable God. Since God is just and equitable, exhibiting His character both in the Cross and the Last Judgment, we must also imitate Him in comparable situations. We must extend grace and love to all, just as our Father does (Mt. 5:44–45), and we must apply the same unmoving standards of justice for all, just as our Father does (Exod. 23:3, 6).

Egalitarian thought, however, makes the assumption that whenever differences are apparent (in income, station, occupation, etc.), the reason for it must be some sort of oppression, an oppression that must be removed by the leveling force of ideological law. Consequently, income is redistributed (through progressive taxation), women are put into combat, children of both sexes play games in city recreation leagues where no one keeps score, and grade inflation afflicts the schools.

There is another contributor to the differences of outcome (because of the fixed standards). Fixed standards have the effect they do because everyone comes to the "starting line" with a different set of God-given desires and abilities. When there is a fixed standard, men and women end differently because men and women begin differently. The same standard—the standard of God's law—applies equally to men and women. Neither are allowed to steal (law), both must call on the Lord for forgiveness (grace), both should have an equal right to a fair trial, and so on. But this does not mean that men and women who come to these same standards are themselves the same.

Men, for example, have a different vocational orientation than women do. Man was made to tend the garden, while woman was made to tend the man: "For the man is not of the woman; but the woman of the man. Neither was the man created for the woman; but the woman for the man" (1 Cor. 11:8–9). The orientation of the husband and wife to one another is therefore different (not better or worse, but different). An illustration I have used before to show this point is the difference between a book written by a woman for women and a book written by a man for men. A book by a man for men is about some mission—winning the battle, finding the gold, getting the rustled cattle back, and so on. When a woman enters the book, what is her role? Well, to help win the battle, find the gold, and the rest of it. But in a book by a woman for women, the relationship *is* the plot. Women are oriented to their husbands, who are oriented to the task or mission.

Because men and women have different desires, they have different temptations. Men, built for conflict, tend to ungodly conflict and rebellion (Rom. 5:12). Women, built to trust, tend to be deceived (1 Tim. 2:14), and, on the flip side of that, to be manipulative (Prov. 7:10). According to the station and resources of each, the temptations come—but we should never forget that their respective virtues line up with the station and resources of each. An example of this would be direct courage (1 Cor. 16:13) and oblique wisdom (Prov. 8:12).

Men and women are also different when it comes to love and respect, as I have touched on briefly in chapter 12. Of course both men and women need love and both men and women need respect, but when the Bible singles out husbands, it tells them to love their wives (Eph. 5:25), and when the Bible singles out wives, it tells them to respect their husbands (Eph. 5:33). We will deal with this in greater depth elsewhere, but this is one of the basic differences between men and women, and it is important to mention it here now. When the Bible tells us to feed the sheep, it is a reasonable inference from this command that sheep need food. In the same way, when it tells wives to respect their husbands, we can infer that one of a man's fundamental needs is to be respected. Similarly, one of a woman's fundamental needs is to be loved. We are commanded to render what God says to render, and not to render what we would like to have gotten or what we think should have been the other person's needs. And keep in mind that if you are not being diligent to render what God says to render, then it will probably be a matter of mere days before you are rendering the opposite. By this I mean caustic acid from husbands instead of warm affection, and castrating disrespect from wives instead of honor.

Forgiveness

Although it is not possible to separate the various aspects of marriage from one another, it is possible to distinguish them. We have come now to the point where we must deal with the fact that marriage means marriage *of* a sinner *to* a sinner. How are we to address marriage and sin? And in order to deal with sin rightly, we have to understand forgiveness, and anyone who wants to be married in this fallen world without understanding forgiveness is frankly out of his mind. Basically, understanding forgiveness means understanding, first, how to receive it, and secondly, how to extend it.

> And grieve not the holy Spirit of God, whereby ye are sealed unto the day of redemption. Let all bitterness, and wrath, and anger, and clamour, and evil speaking, be put away from you, with all malice: and be ye kind one to another, tenderhearted, forgiving one another, even as God for Christ's sake hath forgiven you. (Eph. 4:30–32)

Forgiveness is right at the heart of our Christian calling. In this passage, St. Paul begins by telling us not to grieve the Holy Spirit of God. This command clearly shows that we are not simply obeying a list of impersonal duties but rather we are dealing with a Person, a Person who can be grieved by our behavior. The apostle then gives us a short list of attitudes and behaviors that grieve Him, and he tells us to put them all away. The first is bitterness, followed by two different words for passionate anger and wrath; then comes a word for an uproar or an outcry; next, a word that is literally "blasphemy," meaning in this context "slander" or running somebody down in a grotesque way; and the last is malice, which refers to an ill-will and a desire to injure. Following this list of ways to grieve God, we are given the only alternative: to be kind to one another, tenderhearted, extending mutual forgiveness to one another, just as God forgave us for the sake of Jesus Christ.

The word used here is *charizomai*, meaning both "to bestow graciously" and "to give pardon." How are we to understand this in the context of marriage? First, it is crucial to note that unless both husband and wife understand the principle of forgiveness, their marriage will be described more accurately by verse 31 than by verse 32. And there is nothing worse than a man and woman yoked together whose relationship is characterized by bitterness, anger, uproar, slander, and malice. It is particularly tragic when Christians grieve the Holy Spirit by living this way, when kindness, tender-heartedness, and mutual forgiveness have been offered to them and were all modeled in Christ's gracious reception of us. So, not only does this passage lay out for us the responsibility to forgive, it also gives us the ultimate model of it.

Forgiveness comes from someone whose heart is disposed to kindness and tenderheartedness; we are therefore talking not merely about isolated acts of forgiveness, but also about a deep-rooted disposition to forgive. A forgiving heart is a character trait.

But a forgiving heart can be present and active and yet no forgiveness occurs. How is this possible? This is because forgiveness is a *transaction*. Forgiveness proper occurs when someone approaches someone else and acknowledges that what he did was wrong. He then asks for forgiveness, which is to ask that his behavior will not be held against him. When the person who was approached extends that promise, the transaction of forgiveness is completed. If the forgiver breaks that promise later ("You always do this, just like that time when you . . ."), then he has sinned against the forgiven, and so *he* needs to seek forgiveness. This is the pattern that will usually be followed in a godly marriage, and we will address it in detail in the following section.

Unfortunately, we don't just live in a world where forgiveness is sought and extended whenever it is necessary. We must confront situations (all the time) when forgiveness is necessary but is not sought by the offending party. Now what? The first problem is manifest lack of repentance—we cannot forgive those who are defiant, however much we might like to. Because forgiveness is a transaction, if someone steals your car, you can't run down the street after them, yelling out your forgiveness. But you can have a heart full of forgiveness, full to the brim, ready to overflow the moment repentance appears. Until that happens, there is no forgiveness. We need to distinguish forgiveness in principle and forgiveness accomplished.

But suppose it does happen—the offending party approaches you and earnestly seeks forgiveness—and you discover that in the meantime, your brim-full heart of forgiveness has turned into a brim-full heart of bitterness and resentment. Now the transaction is possible on the other person's end, but because of your bitterness, it is now not possible on your end.

Besides simply a bitter attitude, another problem is suspecting faulty or evil motives of the person seeking forgiveness— "Is he (or she) *really* sorry?" Jesus tells us what our duty is when someone comes to us seven times in one day, seeking forgiveness: each time, Jesus says to forgive (Lk. 17:1–10). Now, on about the third or fourth time, do you think you might be suspicious that your spouse is not really dealing with the issue? Yes, but that does not alter what we are told to do. The forgiveness we are commanded to offer is objective, not based on our feelings or intuitions concerning other people's hearts.

A third difficulty is caused by ignorance. The Bible tells us that love covers a multitude of sins: "And above all things have fervent charity among yourselves: for charity shall cover the multitude of sins. Use hospitality one to another without grudging" (1 Pet. 4:8–9). Notice the context of hospitality here—what sorts of sins are likely to crop up in that situation? The mention of hospitality and grumbling gives us a clue. All of us are guilty of things we are not aware of (especially in marriage), and in any close living situation it is frequently necessary to "let love cover it." This is not, however, the same as "stuffing it" or "eating it." If you eat it, then you must also digest it—and it will turn sour. Letting love cover it, in contrast, is a shortcut to a genuine transaction. But love must either cover it efficaciously or confront it. There is no godly third option.

And last, we come to the problem of the "finger pointed in the wrong direction." This is the central problem in many marriages: "Lord, change him" or "Lord, change her." An accurate awareness of the other's faults does not mean that you yourself are sinless. It is, rather, quite possibly an indication that you are the central problem. Holiness, in wisdom, is aware of the sin of others, but far more common is a markedly unholy awareness of the other's shortcomings which is bitter, wrathful, angry, clamorous, slanderous, and spiteful. Such people often have an eagle-eye—so long as it is looking outward and not inward.

If, by grace, you can overcome these obstacles to forgiveness, you will be greatly blessed by its fruit. Forgiveness makes it possible to "start over," to erase the destructive power of past sins. The power of forgiveness is enormous—the reason it is so infrequently employed is because it transforms everything, and not because it is "a dud." We have already considered what forgiveness is (a transaction), and how to understand it when the other party is being difficult. We now need to look at how forgiveness should work when both husband and wife sincerely want to walk with God and do right by their spouse.

"He that covereth his sins shall not prosper: but whoso confesseth and forsaketh them shall have mercy" (Prov. 28:13). Scripture gives us a contrast between coverings. We tend to be very hesitant to "cover" the sins of others, and very quick to "cover our own." In doing this, we are actually covering our own rear ends and not our sins. But Scripture requires that first desire should be (if possible) to cover the sins of others in love and to refuse to cover our own: "Hatred stirreth up strifes: but love covereth all sins" (Prov. 10:12); "He that covereth a transgression seeketh love; but he that repeateth a matter separateth very friends" (Prov. 17:9). If we fail to obey this wisdom, and take care to cover our own sins, God promises that we will not prosper. But the opposite of self-covering is defined for us in the text itself as *confessing* and *forsaking*, and when this is done, the repentant sinner is promised mercy. The form the mercy takes is defined by the first part of the proverb: the forgiven one shall thrive and prosper.

Now apply this to marriage: are you thriving and prospering in your marriage? We are not asking about income, or reputation, or social status (though all such can be the fruit of prospering); the question is rather one of true fellowship between husband and wife, something that is simply and solely the gift of a gracious God. If you are prospering, then it is because you are not "covering" your own sins in marriage, but rather the sins of the other. If you are not prospering, then it is because your own sin is being covered in some illegitimate fashion, and you and your marriage need to look to the mercy of God.

What, then, is the basic barrier to covering the other's sin instead of our own? We all understand our own frailties very well. It is very unlikely that anyone reading this gets up in the morning and sits down to make a "to do" list, writing on it things like "be short with the kids this afternoon," "be uncommunicative with my wife," or "be disrespectful to my husband." We don't plan these things—they ambush us.

When we wait for the effects of our sin to just "blow over," or we wait to let others "cover it in love," or act like nothing much happened, then our problem is insidious, diabolical, arrogant, marriage-destroying pride. If the sin was major (like an outburst of anger), then the situation demands that we seek forgiveness. To refuse to seek forgiveness is arrogance. If the sin was minor (like irritation in the voice), and we refuse to seek forgiveness, then our pride is so great that we refuse to pick up even a trifle. The former damages directly, and the latter damages by petty insult. For the proud and arrogant, it is either to big to confess or it is too small to confess—nothing is ever just right size to confess. I should note here that although this sort of pride can affect both men and women, it is masculine pride that is far and away the most common offender.

Sometimes the problem is dealing with an intimidating backlog of sins. If you have not lived in your marriage with honest confession of sin, then the chances are good that you have the marital equivalent of a garage that has not been cleaned out for twenty years. The first thing to do is to confess your sins individually (and separately) to God (1 Jn. 1:9). When you are right with Him, then the time is right to make restitution with one another. When you are standing on a high dive, that sensation you feel in your throat is fear. When you are standing on the end of that bouncy board called "humbling yourself," with no water in sight down below, the sensation is also fear—fear fueled by pride.

Once you have dealt with a backlog, your priority must be maintenance. It is always preferable to have a fence at the top of the cliff instead of parking an ambulance at the bottom. One way to build this fence is to keep short accounts. Do not set yourself up for great transgressions by allowing a series of small, presumptuous sins (Ps. 19:13). So here are some suggested house rules that should be agreed upon by husband and wife, and this agreement should be explicit and down to the bone: man and wife should say to one another, "This is the way we want to live together."

First, do not separate, however temporarily, if you are out of fellowship: the husband should not go to work, the wife should not go shopping, and so on. When there is sin between you, dealing with it is the most important priority of your life. This does not mean that you have to fix all the problems that are related to the sin, but you must address the sin itself. Second, do not go into the presence of others when you are out of fellowship: this includes church, parties, Bible studies, or casual visits. This rule also includes not letting anyone into your home when you are out of fellowship: your home should be a place of love and rest, and you do not want any others to ever be ushered into the House of Tension. Third, if the sin occurs when you are around others, arrange a hand signal for putting things right: this should be a simple way of saying, "I was wrong, please forgive me," and "Yes, I do." It should not be so complex, though, that your wife (or anyone else at the gathering) thinks you are telling her to steal third base. Do not, however, merely use such a signal for public sins that were noticed by others—there should not be private apologies for public sins. Finally, do not ever make love when you are out of fellowship: that would make your central union and communion into hypocritical disunion.

Remember too that the "others" here include your children, so if you sin against your wife in front of them, your apology should also be made in front of them. All the rules of thumb given here can be summarized as a simple proverb: "Wash your underwear regularly, and don't do it on the front porch."

15

Divorce

Some people take an approach to marriage that flatters everyone. In other words, it is assumed that everyone wants (deep down) to be a godly husband or a godly wife, and that the only impediment to this marital bliss is ignorance. That ignorance, it turns out, can be remedied with this or that book, seminar, or tape series. This is a fundamentally humanistic view of the situation, and not surprisingly, it is also very naive. Men and women are sinners, and sometimes they don't want to do anything about it. Depending on how grievous the sin is, the question of divorce naturally arises.

> And unto the married I command, yet not I, but the Lord, Let not the wife depart from her husband: But and if she depart, let her remain unmarried, or be reconciled to her husband: and let not the husband put away his wife. But to the rest speak I, not the Lord: If any brother hath a wife that believeth not, and she be pleased to dwell with him, let him not put her away. And the woman which hath an husband that believeth not, and if he be pleased to dwell with her, let her not leave him. For the unbelieving husband is sanctified by the wife, and the unbelieving wife is sanctified by the husband: else were your children unclean; but now are they holy. But if the unbelieving depart, let him depart. A brother or a sister is not under bondage in such cases: but God hath called us to peace. For what knowest thou, O wife, whether thou shalt save thy husband? or how knowest thou, O man, whether thou shalt save thy wife? (1 Cor. 7:10–16)

Many have been confused by St. Paul's language here, assuming that with his "not I, but the Lord," and "I, not the Lord" he is claiming that one part of his letter is inspired by the Holy Spirit and the other part is not. But what he is actually doing is referring to the teaching the Lord gave us during His earthly ministry (vv. 10–11) and then adding his own apostolic teaching to address a new situation that had arisen.

The Lord's teaching presupposes two covenant members. But a new situation had developed as the gospel spread out into the Gentile world, and that was the problem of mixed marriages (vv. 12–13). We are taught here that in the New Covenant, simple unbelief or idolatry on the part of a spouse, in itself, is not grounds for divorce. If the unbeliever is "pleased to dwell with" the believer (*suneudokeo*), then there should be no divorce. This is a hard teaching, and the believer might object: "Paul, think about the kids! Won't this make the children of such a union unholy?" The answer is *no*; the children of such a union are *hagia*, saints (v. 14). But if the unbeliever is not pleased with the godliness of his spouse and leaves, then let him leave. The Christian is not under bondage in such cases. God has called us to peace, so this should not be an occasion for fighting (v. 15). Someone else might say that they "cannot allow the unbeliever to depart" because she still wants to be used as an instrument of his salvation. "But how do you know," St. Paul replies, "whether or not that will happen?" (v. 16). Leave such things in the hand of God.

The Westminster Confession of Faith has a gloriously insightful phrase in talking about marriage and divorce. It says that when it comes to issues of the heart like this, ungodly men are apt "to study arguments." In other words, debates over the lawfulness of divorce are likely to produce a good deal of logic- and text-chopping—and this can happen in both directions. Men and women who want to absolutize marriage run into trouble, and men and women who want to relativize it run into trouble as well.

Marriage is a covenant, and covenants can be broken. Marriage is not an absolute. Marriage is a covenant ordained by God, and so God is the only one who sets the boundaries. What God has joined together let not man put asunder (Mt. 19:6). The thing to be avoided is challenging God. If God requires a divorce, then we ought not attempt keeping together what God has put asunder (Ezra 10). With regard to the absolutizing of marriage, a man who is willing to share his wife with another man is in high rebellion against God and has nothing but contempt for his wife, so that marriage need not be preserved. With regard to the relativizing of marriage, a woman who wants to leave her husband for trivial reasons (say, he doesn't sort the garbage according to her deep desire to recycle) is also in rebellion.

We have no "right" to marital happiness by whatever means necessary (including easy divorce standards). We do have the grace and privilege of joy in the Lord, but this is quite a different thing (Phil. 4:4). This may sound odd to us, but it is only because we have been pounded with secularist propaganda since we were very little. Man is born to trouble as the sparks fly upward, and our troubles vary. Some of us have trouble with our health, others with finances, others with difficult neighbors, and still others have family or marriage troubles. When this happens, God is not wronging us. When we fail to recognize this, our attitude about it often does not help correct the problem; it only fosters more discontent. In the transactions between God and man, man is never shortchanged.

At the same time, St. Paul recognizes the fundamental incompatibility between light and darkness, and he fully realizes that a godly spouse will quite possibly drive off an ungodly one. When this happens, he says, don't worry about it. The believer is not bound in such circumstances. And *not bound* means *not bound*. When a covenant member is the ungodly spouse (in this sense), the result of such overt rebellion should be church discipline, after which he or she is judicially and covenantally to be treated as an unbeliever. In other words, if a Christian man deserts his wife and won't listen to the appeals of the church, then he should be disciplined. Once he is disciplined, he should be regarded as an unbeliever who has deserted a believing spouse, and that believing spouse is now free. Many times, tender-hearted Christians have to learn to hear the words of the apostle here: "Let them depart." As stated earlier, marriage is a covenant union, not some invincible mystic union.

Although God is perfect, He is not a perfectionist. In this passage, the apostle is arguing against a perfectionism that wants to be holier than God. In the course of this he says that an unbeliever, remaining in that unbelief, is not to be divorced provided he is pleased to remain in what the Bible would consider a recognizable marriage. This means that a believing wife or husband is required by Scripture simply to accept the idolatry of his or her spouse. Having said that, the idolatry could get to a level where divorce is required. Consider the detestable practices of the Canaanite wives in Ezra 9–10. In that instance, the unbelief manifested itself in child sacrifice, adultery, and so on. We are not talking about ordinary "Joe non-Christian," the guy with a six-pack in the fridge. Yes, an ordinary pagan (pleased to dwell with his Christian wife) could be quite an ordinary trial to a godly wife. He might curse and swear while working on his car in the garage. He might eat lunch at Hooters every Friday with the guys. He might lose his temper and stomp out of the house sometimes. *Be content,* St. Paul would say. But also remember that relationships (including relationships like this one) are never static. They change and develop over time, and the godly spouse, living in contentment, will be equipped to deal with it.

CHAPTER 16

Marriage and
the Means of Grace

Being a married Christian is a function of simply being a Christian. In other words, we should not expect to find a set of marital "techniques" that are unrelated to the task of living as a Christian generally. For the unmarried, the best preparation for future duties is a pleasant embrace of current duties. For those who are married, there is no way to grow as a husband or wife in Christ apart from growing in Christ period—and so we must consider the means of grace and their effects on marriage.

If ye then be risen with Christ, seek those things which are above, where Christ sitteth on the right hand of God. Set your affection on things above, not on things on the earth. For ye are dead, and your life is hid with Christ in God. When Christ, who is our life, shall appear, then shall ye also appear with him in glory. Mortify therefore your members which are upon the earth; fornication, uncleanness, inordinate affection, evil concupiscence, and covetousness, which is idolatry: For which things' sake the wrath of God cometh on the children of disobedience: In the which ye also walked some time, when ye lived in them. But now ye also put off all these; anger, wrath, malice, blasphemy, filthy communication out of your mouth. Lie not one to another, seeing that ye have put off the old man with his deeds; And have put on the new man, which is renewed in knowledge after the image of him that created him. (Col. 3:1–10)

In this text, we have all the ingredients of a lousy marriage, as well as instruction that, if followed, will make your marriage a blessed relationship. What does your baptism mean? What does it point to? If you have been raised with Christ, then look to the heavens because you have also ascended with Him (v. 1). Set your affection on heavenly things, not earthly things (v. 2). The reason for this is that you are dead in Christ (with regard to worldly things), and your life is in the heavenlies with Christ (v. 3). When Christ, our life, comes again, we shall be glorified in Him (v. 4). This being the case, and on this basis, St. Paul tells Christians to put certain things to death, that is, their earthly members.

Those members are fornication (sexual impurity), uncleanness (having a dirty body and mind), inordinate affection (no emotional balance), lust, and coveting what is your neighbor's (whether it be his house, car, wife, or daughter), for that is idolatry (v. 5). God hates all of these things and is angry with those who practice them (v. 6). Many Christians used to be pagans and remember this way of life (v. 7). Finally, we are also told to put off attitudinal and verbal problems—anger, wrath, malice, blasphemy, filthy talk, and lies (vv. 8–9). Having put off the old carcass, we are to put on the new man, the Lord Jesus Christ (v. 10).

Sometimes those in the Reformed tradition have tended to emphasize our remaining sinfulness to such an extent that we begin to exhibit a stubborn willfulness about it. While a casual and breezy perfectionism is of course to be rejected—and rejected with loathing—it remains the case that God commands us to be *done* with sin. We are not to live that way, and we are not to wallow in faithless self-flagellation, convincing ourselves that we still live that way despite God's grace. We are called to put off sin and put on Christ.

There are two ways of looking at our text. One emphasizes that it tells Christians to mortify their members which are on the earth, and that it says those members are inherently sinful. This is quite true, but it is also true that the point of the command is to *mortify* those members. How we respond to God's commands in such matters makes a difference. There is such a thing as righteousness on the earth and righteousness within marriage. It is not the case that a backslidden Christian is under one hundred feet of water, and the godliest saint who ever lived is only under three feet of water, but both of them are equally wet. Rather, obedience and disobedience, or faithfulness and unfaithfulness, are two different states. True obedience is possible, and God expects it. The yoke of Christ is easy and His burden is light (Mt. 11:30).

At the same time, we should not underestimate sin either—we do struggle with our remaining sinfulness, and we will do so, to some extent, until we are with the Lord. Do not look for convenience-store holiness. The great Puritan John Owen said that a man will make no progress in godliness unless he walks daily over the bellies of his lusts. Let he who thinks he stands take heed lest he fall (1 Cor. 10:12).

First, for all those who are in Christ, the old man is dead (Rom. 6:6). This was done definitively at conversion (by God, and not by us), and does not need to be repeated. It *cannot* be repeated. Second, for those who are already in Christ, our attachments to the world through our members must be mortified or executed, as in our passage from Colossians (cf. Rom. 6:12–13). The Greek verb for "mortify" here is an aorist imperative—in other words, it's telling you to put it to death and walk away from the carcass with your revolver smoking. This thing, when done, is to be definitively done. Third, you will continue to deal with remaining sinfulness the rest of your life. Complacency is deadly. You might weed your garden every summer for twenty years, but what will happen if you then quit for just one summer? Rather, at all times abstain from fleshly lusts, which war against your soul (1 Pet. 2:11).

This brings us to consider some of the specific sins mentioned in our Colossians passage, sins which are very much marriage-killers. Husbands and wives who do not mortify their "members which are on the earth" are actively engaged in an attempted mortification of their marriage. This is another "not whether, but which" situation. It is not whether you will mortify something; it is which thing you will mortify. What will it be: your sin or your marriage?

In the text from Colossians, the prime marriage-killers are these: (1) *Sexual covetousness and lust:* Too many Christian men are not serious enough about dealing with this, and too many Christian wives behave in that prim and fussy way they have that ensures their husband will never enlist their help. (2) *Anger:* Far from being the hidden sin, this is explosive and out in the open (at least within the family). In this passage, we also see that anger is often connected with "blasphemy." (3) *Lies:* Often, these household lies are covered with euphemisms to make them acceptable—"discrete silence," "manners," and so on. (4) *Covetousness:* How many wives urge their husbands to the wrong kind of ambition?

So how do you mortify these sins? How do you "pull the trigger?" The answer is simple on one level—repentance and faith. You decide that you are done with the sin (repentance). You change your mind about it. You do this in the context of what God has provided for your strengthening (faith). What is that context? It is worship, confession, Scripture-reading, prayer, thanksgiving, psalm-singing, and taking the Lord's Supper. Christians must present themselves before the Lord on the first day of the week, and they must do so in order to renew covenant with Him. All our spiritual exercises during the course of the week are to prepare us for worship, and in this worship we meet with God in order to glorify Him, and in order that He might strengthen us. A husband and a wife who are struggling with sin in their marriage must resolve together to be worshipping Christians, and they must give themselves to learning what they need to learn in order to worship effectively. As they do this, God really does renew His covenant with them weekly, and He really does strengthen and nourish them. They are being grown up into Christ, the perfect man, and this has a direct impact on how they treat one another on Monday morning.

Study Your Spouse

Learning is awkward. Even assuming good motives, a desire to learn, and no basic rebellion against God's pattern, there are still difficulties. G. K. Chesterton once said that the "chief object of education is not to learn things but to unlearn things." Couple this with the fact that what we must unlearn is frequently what we have assumed to be virtuous, and the magnitude of the problem becomes apparent.

> Likewise, ye husbands, dwell with them according to knowledge, giving honour unto the wife, as unto the weaker vessel, and as being heirs together of the grace of life; that your prayers be not hindered. (1 Pet. 3:7)

> [T]hat they may teach the young women to be sober, to love their husbands . . . (Tit. 2:4)

In these texts we find the common element of learning or study. The husband is commanded to live with his wife *according to knowledge* (1 Pet. 3:7), and the older women are required to *teach* the younger women how, among other things, to be husband-lovers (Tit. 2:4). Putting this in very simple terms, husbands are commanded to be students of their wives, and wives are commanded to be students of their husbands. Being a husband or a wife is a high vocational calling, and you would not walk into any *lesser* job or vocation with no expectation of needing to be trained.

Something that good teachers have in common is knowing how to anticipate what the student *thinks* he needs to do, so they can show him what he must do *instead* of that. This is true whether you are learning to play the guitar, drive a car, or do a math problem. What feels intuitively right falls under the heading of what your coach calls a "common mistake." It is no different in learning how to live with a man or a woman.

As we consider the difficulties of fighting the ignorance of husbands and wives, remember that we have already considered the difficulties involved in fighting sin. We are not forgetting that here, but rather assuming it. Even if you succeed in keeping the weeds from growing three feet high, and diligently respond to each appearance of new weeds, there are additional difficulties in growing a garden—difficulties that require education more than repentance. But if you don't deal with sin first, you will never have the privilege of experiencing those additional difficulties.

So, apart from sin, why is it that learning to live with your spouse can be awkward? There are several things to keep in mind here: men and women think and respond differently; different individuals and personalities think and respond differently; many of us have not been taught well in this regard, and so we do the wrong thing, assuming it to be the right thing; and we are too impatient with the process—but making a bottle of fine wine is a very different thing than mixing up a jug of fruit juice.

Taking all these things into account, here are some biblical principles that will enable you to embrace the difficulties as part of what God has designed for you—and to embrace them wisely, not as some kind of a marital masochist. Marriage is a marathon, not a sprint. Keep your eye on the goal, and have a realistic view of what the goal actually is: "Now no chastening for the present seemeth to be joyous, but grievous: nevertheless afterward it yieldeth the peaceable fruit of righteousness unto them which are exercised thereby" (Heb. 12:11).

Imputing motives is a bad idea. Because you are different, it does not work well to reason thusly—"If *I* had done something like that, my motives would have been thus and such. *He* did that. Therefore, his motives must have been thus and such." Telepathy in marriage doesn't work any better than it does anywhere else. "Counsel in the heart of man is like deep water; but a man of understanding will draw it out" (Prov. 20:5).

Question hidden assumptions. Your assumptions about what constitutes being a godly spouse are often poor assumptions. For example, many men simply assume that since they are to love their wives, they should demonstrate this by working eighty hours a week to make a good income for them. Bad idea. Likewise, many women think that since God gave her to him as a helpmeet, she must therefore be the chairman of the Husband Reform Committee. Equally bad idea: "man doth not live by bread only, but by every word that proceedeth out of the mouth of the Lord doth man live" (Deut. 8:3). We are to live by what God actually said, and not by what we think it would have been good of Him to have said.

Don't let external problems affect the relationship. Too many people confound arguing with their spouse and arguing with reality—many marital frustrations and squabbles are quarrels with gravity and not quarrels with sin. Because of our frustration with gravity, we too often project sin on to the other person. This happens when a man yells at his wife because he has to change a flat tire, or when a wife is sharp with her husband because she just found out that her best friend's husband in Oklahoma was unfaithful.

Differences are not an insult. We are Trinitarians, and one of the chief blessings that should flow from this doctrine is the ability to enjoy one another *for being other*. Too often, we only want to enjoy superficial differences, but we do not want the differences that go all the way down to the bone. Men enjoy the fact that their wives are physiologically different but don't like the fact that their entire mental and emotional framework is also different. Men too often want a man's brain in a woman's body, and women do the same thing—wanting someone who is tough and manly on the outside but with a heart made of goo pudding. Embracing differences out of trinitarian principle includes both gender differences and personality differences: "That they all may be one; as thou, Father, art in me, and I in thee, that they also may be one in us: that the world may believe that thou hast sent me" (Jn. 17:21).

CHAPTER

18

Love and Respect

As we have seen, the central command given to husbands as husbands in the New Testament is the command to *love*, and the central command given to wives as wives is the command to honor and respect. Let's consider this difference in more detail.

> For the husband is the head of the wife, even as Christ is the head of the church: and he is the saviour of the body. Therefore as the church is subject unto Christ, so let the wives be to their own husbands in every thing. Husbands, love your wives, even as Christ also loved the church, and gave himself for it; That he might sanctify and cleanse it with the washing of water by the word, That he might present it to himself a glorious church, not having spot, or wrinkle, or any such thing; but that it should be holy and without blemish. So ought men to love their wives as their own bodies. He that loveth his wife loveth himself. For no man ever yet hated his own flesh; but nourisheth and cherisheth it, even as the Lord the church. (Eph. 5:23–29)

We are not told that the husband *ought* to be the head of the wife, but rather that he *is* (v. 23). A man may be a faithful head or an unfaithful head, but in either case he is a head. Here St. Paul is urging husbands to be faithful heads, as saviors to the body (v. 23). Wives are to be subject to their husbands in everything, as the Church is subject to Christ (v. 24). Then Paul gives the central command to husbands—love your wives, as Christ loved the Church and gave Himself for it (v. 25). The result of this self-gift is that the Church would be sanctified and cleansed by the washing of water by the Word (v. 26), and the result of this baptismal washing, made efficacious by the word heard in faith, is that the Church will be glorious and unblemished (v. 27). In the same way, husbands ought to love their wives as their own bodies (v. 28); a man who loves his wife loves himself (v. 28). Nobody ever hated his own body, but nourishes and cherishes it—as the Lord does with the Church (v. 29).

Among conservative, family-oriented Christians, this passage is familiar territory. But because of what St. Paul actually says here, we will spend the rest of our lives learning from it, and even then we will not come close to all that it contains. The first thing to note is that love means gift—sacrificial gift. Love is not love if it refuses to give; neither is it love when a man gives *things* as a substitute for having to give *himself.* True husbandly love is rendered when a man gives himself to the uttermost, and then as a result of that self-gift, he naturally gives other things (material provision) as well. A man cannot bestow himself and then not bestow provision, protection, and so on, but a man can bestow provision and not bestow himself.

In this men are called to imitate God. God so loved the world that He gave Himself in His Son (Jn. 3:16), and Christ loved the Church and gave Himself for it (Eph. 5:25). This self-gift is tantamount to death. You men are not told to be prepared in principle to die for your wives *if* the occasion ever calls for it—but since you live in the security of the suburbs, it probably won't. Every husband is called to give himself away, and this is a death. But in the glorious purposes of God, it is a death *and resurrection.* He who loves his wife (death) loves himself (life again). Jesus endured the cross—for the joy that was set before Him. In this, be sure to distinguish death from dying. Men are not told to be in perpetual death-bed agonies for their wives. We are not told to twist in the wind. Dying can just be a form of miserable living and is no help to anybody in your family. Do the whole thing and die, and what

God will raise up is glorious. In short, husbands are to lay down their lives and not make a show of laying down their lives in such a way as to get their wives to pity them.

This kind of love is efficacious. Obviously, husbands cannot reenact the substitutionary atonement for the sins of the world, and no one associated with the publication of this book thinks that they can. But they are commanded to imitate it—and to imitate it with an eye on the results. In this, as with everything else, the results are God's. This is God's pattern of action, the way of God. This is just the kind of thing that He would use.

When a man loves a woman unto death (in every sense), God uses that love to sanctify, cleanse, wash, nourish, and cherish her. And just as Christ loves His bride to the end of her ultimate loveliness, so husbands are commanded to love their wives into loveliness—because God has determined that such a self-gift bestows loveliness. In other words, love bestows loveliness; love comes before loveliness. What carnal men believe to be the horse is actually the cart. We love God (and are therefore lovely) because He *first* loved us (1 Jn. 4:19), and God showed His love for us in this: while we were yet sinners, Christ died for us (Rom. 5:8).

Men must not love their wives solely because they are lovely—although wise and loving fathers will give young, fathead bridegrooms a head start. Men must not love their wives only if their wives "keep themselves up." As a wise Puritan put it, men must choose their love and then must love their choice. As they love their choice, they bestow loveliness—the covenantal responsibility and burden of the wife's loveliness therefore resides with the husband. Husbands do not do this by becoming her hairdresser or make-up artist; they do it by bestowing the gift of self-sacrifice. This gift aims at the inner beauty (that beauty which is of great worth in God's sight), but every other aspect of life (including a wife's external countenance and loveliness) flows naturally from that.

This is a great mystery. We cannot do the math. We do not know how God brings about this particular harvest of loveliness, but He does. Husbands, after five years of living with you, does that blessing register on your wife's face? What about after ten years? Twenty?

One last word on this to husbands: The message of death and resurrection is *gospel*, not super-law. This is not condemnation. The man who loves his wife loves himself.

So husbands are commanded to love, and we are taught that the love they are to render is the kind that bestows loveliness. But wives are not encouraged by this to simply be passive recipients—they are given a command as well. They are to be subject to their husbands (Eph. 5:24), and they are to honor and reverence their own husbands (v. 33). We find the same counterintuitive principle at work here, because just as love bestows loveliness, so also respect bestows respectability.

> Wives, submit yourselves unto your own husbands, as unto the Lord. For the husband is the head of the wife, even as Christ is the head of the church: and he is the saviour of the body. Therefore as the church is subject unto Christ, so let the wives be to their own husbands in every thing. . . . This is a great mystery: but I speak concerning Christ and the church. Nevertheless let every one of you in particular so love his wife even as himself; and the wife see that she reverence her husband. (Eph. 5:22–24, 32–33)

In some sense, the relationship between husband and wife is like the relationship between Christ and the Church. Consequently, husbands are commanded to model themselves after the pattern of Jesus Christ, and in a reciprocal way, wives are commanded to model themselves after the Church. They are in the first place to submit themselves to their own husbands as to the Lord (v. 22). Just as the Church is subject to Christ, so wives are to be this way to their husbands in everything (v. 24). There is no great mystery at all in men browbeating their wives, but *this* is a great mystery (v. 32). So husbands are to love, and wives are to reverence their own husbands (v. 33). As we shall show, this does not reduce women to a state of helplessness, but rather to a true feminine authority.

This begins with evangelical death. As we noted regarding the charge to husbands, it is not possible to improve oneself through fits and starts; the Christian pattern of self-improvement is to die and rise. The same thing is true of the Church. Just as Jesus died for the Church, so everyone in the Church is called to take up the cross and follow Him. Wives are equally summoned to fulfill this pattern by mortifying their own desires for autonomy. The pattern is not "husbands die, wives coast." Each is summoned to die, so that they might be raised to their particular calling.

With this in mind, let's take a closer look at some of the words. Wives are to "submit" themselves (*hupotasso*, v. 22). The word is a Greek military term and means to subject, submit, or subordinate oneself to a line of authority. The same word is used in verse 24 (cf. 1 Pet. 3:1). In Titus 2:5, the same word is rendered as "obedient." In Ephesians 5:33, wives are told to reverence their own husbands (*phobeo*). In this context, it carries the sense of "awe, honor, and respect," and not the idea of being scared or having a phobia (the same thing is true in 1 Peter 3:2).

A few other words from elsewhere in the New Testament help fill out the picture. Sarah was subject to her own husband (*hupotasso*, 1 Pet. 3:5), and in the next verse it says that Sarah obeyed her husband (*hupakouo*, v. 6), calling him lord (*kurios*, v. 6). Peter tells Christian wives that they are her daughters if they do what is right and do not give way to fear. The word *hupakouo* comes from the duties of a porter, who was to listen attentively at the door for an inquiring knock. In 1 Timothy 2:9, the word *aidos* urges women to a deferential reverence.

Wives should first make sure they clearly understand the actual standard. The fact that your husband is to love you sacrificially does not alter the content of what this enables and requires you to do. This applies even when he is not acting in all wisdom. Husbands are prohibited from bluster, bossing about, selfish grasping, and all the rest of it, but the Bible nevertheless requires wives to obey their husbands. This obedience is to be cheerful, complete, reverent, all the way down, and across the board. Remember that in our passage St. Paul tells wives to be subject to their husbands "in every thing." Now I am fully aware that in our current cultural climate this is a perfectly outrageous thing to say and teach. It may even be illegal in some states. This is too bad, because the grass withers and the flower fades, but the Word of the Lord endures forever.

You have heard the qualification about this many times—no human authority is absolute, and if your husband commands you to break God's law, then you must (*submissively*) decline to do so. But this is almost never where the problem is.

In order to do submit rightly, a woman must die and be raised again. But why is submission a form of dying? Why can this be hard for women to do? In Genesis 4:6–7, Cain is told that sin lies in wait for him and desires to master him, but he must rule over it. This is a very unusual combination of words in Hebrew, and the only other place it is found is in the previous chapter, where Eve is told that her desire will be for her husband, but that he will rule over her (Gen. 3:16). Part of the fallen order is women's desire to run their husbands in an ungodly way, in big things and little things. But Jesus came to deal with this. He enables Christian women to partake in His suffering and death, and He raises them up again.

Many people fear that this teaching will turn women into doormats, fit only to be walked over by abusive men, but in fact the very opposite is the case. Remember that love bestows loveliness—if a man sacrifices himself in a Christ-like way, laying down his life for his wife in issues great and small, what is her natural response? Is it "Oh, good, now I can get really fat. Pass the chocolates"? Not at all—love bestowed bestows loveliness. Similarly, respect bestows respectability. Honor bestows honor. Reverence bestows dignity. The God who made the reciprocity of the sexes included this feature in it as well. On average, men who are respected do not collapse into "Oh, good, now I get to be disreputable"—any more than women who are loved think of it as an opportunity to become slovenly.

The call to men and women both is quite simple: to *bestow* and *give*, not *take* and *grab*.

Wise Words in Marriage

James tells us that the tongue is an unruly member. If we can control the tongue, he says, we can control anything. At the same time, the Bible teaches that the tongue has tremendous power for good. With our words we are able both to build and to destroy.

> The wise in heart shall be called prudent: and the sweetness of the lips increaseth learning. Understanding is a wellspring of life unto him that hath it: but the instruction of fools is folly. The heart of the wise teacheth his mouth, and addeth learning to his lips. Pleasant words are as an honeycomb, sweet to the soul, and health to the bones. (Prov. 16:21–24)

Let us consider this passage in the context of marriage. The wise in *heart* are known as prudent, and their speech is sweet and edifying (v. 21). Notice the general flow—from heart to mouth. Wisdom in the heart leads to sweetness on the lips, which in turn causes others to learn (v. 21). Understanding, like wisdom, is also in the heart, and it is described as a wellspring of life, bubbling up (v. 22). But what bubbles up out of the heart of the fool? Folly. The mouth of a wise man is instructed by his heart (v. 23). Moreover, his heart adds learning to his lips, which amounts to a reinforcement of the same thing (v. 23). Pleasant words are a honeycomb, going down to the soul and down to the bones (v. 24). Notice that wisdom in this passage goes from the inside to the outside, and then it travels from the outside back down to the

bones of others. Pleasant words are the words of the pure (Prov.
15:26). To apply this for our purposes, pleasant words are sweet
to the soul *of your marriage*, and they are health to the bones *of
your marriage*.

Words are not abstract entities with an ethereal life of their
own in Dictionary Heaven. Biblically considered, words are spoken in a particular place at a particular time, and full understanding is only possible for those who by grace understand the world
in this same way. Words in this respect are like the Word. "And
the Word was made flesh, and dwelt among us" (Jn. 1:14a). The
glory of words is therefore revealed only when they are enfleshed
and particularized. This means that words were given to us in order to be set in place like fine jewelry: "A word fitly spoken is like
apples of gold in pictures of silver. As an earring of gold, and an
ornament of fine gold, so is a wise reprover upon an obedient ear"
(Prov. 25:11–12). "A man hath joy by the answer of his mouth:
and a word spoken in due season, how good is it!" (Prov. 15:23).
"The lips of the righteous know what is acceptable: but the mouth
of the wicked speaketh frowardness" (Prov. 10:32).

Since words only gain full meaning when set in a specific
context, husbands and wives must learn to speak to one another
carefully—but there are two kinds of "carefully." You should not
have to be careful because you are handling a high explosive that
might go off at any time. Rather, you should be careful because
you are a jeweler of words—you are setting fourteen-carat words
in their appropriate place, and when you are done, it will be
worth ten thousand dollars. This is the right kind of "carefully."

When harmful (or unhelpful) words are spoken, only the
most hardened sinner flatly denies having said what everyone
heard him say. Instead, the speaker of such words resorts to spin
control. Each sentence has a simple message—that is, the meaning which can be ascertained by a Chinese student of English
through careful use of a Random House dictionary. Unfortunately, this denotative meaning of the sentence is only a small
fraction of what is being communicated. Each sentence also has

what one author has called a *meta-message*, and which I would call its *symbolic context*.[1] This is where the real action is. The symbolic context of your words includes your past, your ancestors, your face, your tone, your silences, and where you place your accents. Take, for example, the sentence "We are having lasagna tonight," and put a certain accent on it: "We are having *lasagna* tonight?" When overlaying meanings like this causes trouble, a favorite way of defending yourself is the grievous sin of "pleading the dictionary." This is using the symbolic context to get your hook in, and then retreating to the dictionary to defend yourself when your spouse counterattacks you for your unkindness. For our example, it would sound something like this: "When did I ever *say* I didn't like your lasagna?" Trying to do this is a formal denial of the incarnate value of your words and the meaning that surrounds your every utterance. On a very real and practical level, it is an attempt to deny the Incarnation.

So we must be diligent students of words in our marriages, understanding all the nuances of our speech. But there are many other lessons for us in this area, and what follows is a short list compiled from the wisdom of Proverbs.

First, good communication in marriage is not necessarily a function of quantity. Endless chatter can be harmful: "In the multitude of words there wanteth not sin: but he that refraineth his lips is wise" (Prov. 10:19). "He that hath knowledge spareth his words: and a man of understanding is of an excellent spirit. Even a fool, when he holdeth his peace, is counted wise: and he that shutteth his lips is esteemed a man of understanding" (Prov. 17:27–28). Good communication in marriage is not hasty: "Seest thou a man that is hasty in his words? there is more hope of a fool than of him" (Prov. 29:20). Good communication in marriage does not have to defend itself with "you started it!"—it takes two to tangle: "A soft answer turneth away wrath: but grievous

---

[1] See Deborah Tannen, *I Only Say This Because I Love You* (New York: Random House, 2001).

words stir up anger" (Prov. 15:1). Good communication in marriage knows what the other person would say because communication is not just speaking—it is speaking *and hearing*: "Wherefore, my beloved brethren, let every man be *swift to hear*, slow to speak, slow to wrath" (Jas. 1:19). Good communication is jealous and discrete: "The words of a talebearer are as wounds, and they go down into the innermost parts of the belly" (Prov. 18:8; 26:22).

The dangers in communication are great, but the blessings far outweigh them. Wouldn't it be nice to have your marriage watered by a well of life? "The mouth of a righteous man *is a well of life*" (Prov. 10:11a), and "A wholesome tongue is *a tree of life*" (Prov. 15:4). Every husband and every wife is called to be diligently biblical in their everyday use of words. This means diligent biblical application to the practical theology of language. "Bow down thine ear, and hear the words of the wise, and apply thine heart unto my knowledge. For it is a pleasant thing if thou keep them within thee; they shall withal be fitted in thy lips" (Prov. 22:17–18).

PART IV:
Marriage is Good

CHAPTER
20

Food, Glorious Food

The family that eats together stays together. Food is very important in the edification of a marriage and family, and to see its importance, we should begin at the beginning.

> So God created man in his own image, in the image of God created he him; male and female created he them. And God blessed them, and God said unto them, Be fruitful, and multiply, and replenish the earth, and subdue it: and have dominion over the fish of the sea, and over the fowl of the air, and over every living thing that moveth upon the earth. And God said, Behold, I have given you every herb bearing seed, which is upon the face of all the earth, and every tree, in the which is the fruit of a tree yielding seed; to you it shall be for meat. And to every beast of the earth, and to every fowl of the air, and to every thing that creepeth upon the earth, wherein there is life, I have given every green herb for meat: and it was so. (Gen. 1:27–30)

We see in the first place that God created man (mankind) in His own image. We are told this twice in two different ways, and the writer of this passage goes out of his way to note that male and female *together* constitute this image (v. 27). Having created them, God blessed them and gave them their marching orders: (1) be fruitful, (2) multiply, (3) replenish the earth, (4) subdue the earth, and (5) exercise dominion over all living creatures. In short, the man and woman were told to increase their numbers fruitfully. They were told to restore to the earth what they had taken from it. They were told to subdue the earth, and they were told to rule the animals. All this was a tall order—quite enough to make you hungry. So God gave them every herb-bearing seed and all fruit-bearing trees so that they might eat. After the Flood, God included meat on the menu (Gen. 9:2–3). So this is the creational order in our passage: God *created* them, He *blessed* them, He *charged* them, and He *fed* them.

This great creation mandate was not undone by the effects of sin. Immediately after history's greatest judgment on sin, the Flood, God renews this cultural mandate with some modifications. Sin has never altered the task assigned to man, but it has destroyed our ability to fulfill it. The coming of Christ addressed this shortcoming rather than being an instance of God giving up on the task. After the coming of Christ, we now see the only possibility of fulfilling the task.

> For unto the angels hath he not *put in subjection the world to come*, whereof we speak. But one in a certain place testified, saying, What is man, that thou art mindful of him? or the son of man, that thou visitest him? Thou madest him a little lower than the angels; thou crownedst him with glory and honour, *and didst set him over the works of thy hands: Thou hast put all things in subjection under his feet.* For in that he put all in subjection under him, he left nothing that is not put under him. *But now we see not yet all things put under him. But we see Jesus,* who was made a little lower than the angels for the suffering of death, crowned with glory and honour; that he by the grace of God should taste death for every man. (Heb. 2:5–9)

We do not see everything put under us, and neither did Adam. We do see numerous instances of failure—the earth refusing to be subdued (Rom. 8:19–21). The author of Hebrews says that he is talking about the subjection of the world to come (the age to come, in which we now live), and he is talking about the subjection of that world *in Christ:* "But we see Jesus . . ." (v. 9).

Now remember the pattern from Genesis: God creates us, blesses us, charges us, and feeds us. We have the same (and greater) privileges in the New Covenant. God has re-created us in the new creation (2 Cor. 5:17); God blesses us in that new creation (Rev. 22:14); God has given us something to do, which amounts to the same charge given in Genesis (Mt. 28:18–20); and God gives us strength for our assigned task by feeding us (Jn. 6:35).

This is all glorious, but let's make it practical—let's get our feet under the table. How does all this apply to marriage? Remember, first "male and female created he them," and then, in *that* particular context, God blessed, charged and fed them. And in this biblical context, we need to realize that if half our meals are eaten over the sink, then something is wrong. How should we arrange our meals, the food we receive from God, in an appropriate hierarchy? Husbands and wives must beware of the temptation to gear all meals to the kids, and so together they should do the following:

Feed on Christ's words. As Jesus talks about feeding on Him as the bread of heaven, He places this in a context that emphasizes the importance of feeding on His words: "It is the spirit that quickeneth; the flesh profiteth nothing: the words that I speak unto you, they are spirit, and they are life" (Jn. 6:63).

Feed on Christ's body. "The cup of blessing which we bless, is it not the communion of the blood of Christ? The bread which we break, is it not the communion of the body of Christ? For we being many are one bread, and one body: for we are all partakers of that one bread" (1 Cor. 10:16–17). And of course this is done by faith alone. We chew and swallow by believing, and because we believe Christ, we actually chew and swallow. One of the great needs of the hour in our churches is a restoration of the Lord's Supper to the central place that Reformers like John Calvin wanted for it. This is another subject for another book, but Christian families really need to be communing families.

Feast in our households on the Lord's Day. The Sabbath is a feast day, not a fasting day (Lev. 23:1–3), and it is a feast that extends into "all your dwellings." Similarly, the meal in the church is called by the apostle a festival (1 Cor. 5:8), and the Lord's brother says the same (Jude 12). One of the most pernicious forms of Sabbath-breaking is this: "Once every seven days God expects us to get chintzy for Him." But not surprisingly, this attitude spreads throughout the rest of our lives, especially our meals at home. But when we embrace the festival of worship, this festival works its way into our homes.

Pray for and receive our daily bread with thanksgiving. The Lord taught us to pray for our daily bread (Mt. 6:11). The apostle Paul tells us that every french fry at every fast food emporium must be consumed to the glory of God (1 Cor. 10:31).

Now what this means is that the "nutrition" from each kind of eating will cascade down to the other kinds of eating below. As we hear in faith, we will come to the Lord's Table in faith. As we come to the Lord's Table in faith, learning how to eat together with *His* family, we will be enabled to gather together on the Lord's Day to eat with our *own* families. As we honor the Lord on His day in our households, we will find that our own meals begin to grow and mature.

Growing Old Together

One of the hardest lessons for an egalitarian age to learn is how to render honor. As we seek to correct this, though, we must remember that this honor must not be worldly or carnal—we are called to render honor as understood in a biblical and Christian way. And since age is important to the biblical idea of honor, we can make direct applications to how husbands and wives are to grow old together.

> Thou shalt rise up before the hoary head, and honour the face of the old man, and fear thy God: I am the LORD. (Lev. 19:32)

> The hoary head is a crown of glory, if it be found in the way of righteousness. (Prov. 16:31)

As men and women grow old together, many people's natural response is pity. Because the elderly can't "keep up" anymore, they are thought of as society's stragglers. Sometimes this comes out in exasperation (on the freeway, when we're behind somebody in geezer drive), and other times in pity, but the root assumption is the same. A biblical approach, in contrast, would suggest that the elderly among us are the vanguard rather than stragglers. All of us will one day rise, but before we rise, we will all die. Death really is an enemy (1 Cor. 15:55), but it is an enemy that we are besieging, and the elderly among us are at the top of our siege ladders, ready to go over the top of the wall first. The dead in Christ will rise *first* (1 Thes. 4:16), and then those who are alive.

This is one reason why our fundamental and natural response toward the elderly should be one of honor. We can express this honor externally by standing when a gray head enters the room and by rising to honor the face of the elderly. This is part of what it means to fear God. But like everything else in this fallen world (given the presence of sin), it is not automatic. A gray head is a crown of glory—provided that gray head is found in the way of righteousness (Prov. 16:31). Now let us relate this to marriage. Children are taught to honor their father and mother in their advanced years (Mk. 7:9–13), and this honor toward two gray heads is to be practical and tangible. Further, it cannot be trumped by some false sense of spirituality.

We tend to separate family issues systematically—marriage issues on the one hand and children/parent issues on the other. But ultimately, in covenant life, these things can be distinguished but not separated. This means that parents have a responsibility to bring their children up in such a way that they learn what it means to honor father and mother (Eph. 6:1–4). Little children render honor through cheerful obedience. Grown children render it through practical support, among other ways (Mk. 7:9–13).

Now the fundamental way your children learn how to honor you the way they are supposed to is the same way we learn all valuable lessons—imitation. They learn by watching you with *your* parents, the parents of both husband and wife. Honor demanded downstream is a poor substitute for honor rendered upstream. A husband and wife should say, "We should honor our parents so that it will go well with our children." They ought not say, "Our children should honor their parents (which turns out to be us!) so that it will go well with us." This may seem just like a slight difference, but it is the distance between heaven and hell. If you are given to excuses and rationalizations with regard to your parents, do you really think there will be no such excuses available to your children thirty years from now?

Having said this, it is also important to remember the ever-present distinction between principles and methods. Sometimes constant medical care is necessary, for example, and a nursing home is unavoidable. But all faithful family members should be able to tell at a glance the difference between abandoned and loved, and all outsiders should remember the difference between having all the facts and not having them.

It may also be helpful to note the difference between general principles, which apply to most believers in most cases, and specific moral requirements, which apply to each and every believer, head for head, all the time. As part of the moral law, for example, all believers are commanded to avoid adultery. An example of a general principle, however, might be that a man should provide for his own household, unless providentially hindered (1 Tim. 5:8). Similarly, the Bible tells us, as a general principle, that a righteous man leaves an inheritance for his children's children (Prov. 13:22), and the apostle Paul points to the same general reality when he says that he does not want to be burdensome to the Corinthians: "for I seek not yours, but you: for the children ought not to lay up for the parents, but the parents for the children" (2 Cor. 12:14b). Married couples need to honor and care for their parents, while equipping their own children to do the same for them.

Another issue in aging marriages is the effect of time on small sins. Being married happily is a skilled and difficult art, and when you are young you might believe you can afford to be "a little off." But two lines a quarter of an inch apart on your first anniversary can be three yards apart by your fiftieth. Time alone does not solve that kind of problem. All the issues we have been addressing in this series on marriage are issues that (unresolved) can only be accentuated over time: bitterness, lust, abdication, usurpation, and so on. Feeding the cockroaches is not a good long-term strategy, even if they spend *most* of their time out of sight behind and under the cupboards. Keep short accounts, and time will have no chance to amplify your (initially small) sins.

Aging marriages should bring marital wisdom, and as we have already noted, this wisdom should be taught to the next generation. Older women are expected to know how to live with a man, and they should be able to pass that wisdom on (Tit. 2:4). In a similar way, elders should know how to manage a household well (1 Tim. 3:4). Living this way in wisdom is something the men and women can know how to do. Some know, and some do not. Those who do not know how to live this way (which includes some old people, and all young people) are obligated as Christian disciples to learn how. Living wisely is not accomplished by simply doing "what comes naturally." This is a fallen world, and sin comes naturally. So do divorces.

Finally, contentment is for life. The Bible teaches that old age is not for sissies (Eccl. 12:1–7). Various afflictions come with old age, and the Scriptures teach us what to do in the course of all afflictions. We are to rejoice and be grateful (Phil. 4:11–13). In the intimacy of marriage, your spouse will know the most about what you are having to deal with, and he or she should also know the most about your joy when you meet with these various trials (Jas. 1:2ff). It's important to keep some perspective here—one of the reasons we experience so many of these afflictions on such a wide scale is that so many of us today are living so much longer. We are now discovering all kinds of "old-people problems"—and even this should be grounds for gratitude.

CHAPTER 22

Widowhood

The usually cynical Ambrose Bierce defined a widow in this way: "A pathetic figure that the Christian world has agreed to take humorously, although Christ's tenderness towards widows was one of the most marked features of his character." James tells us that pure and undefiled religion involves visiting widows (Jas. 1:27), and a moment's reflection should reveal the importance of understanding the role of widows (and widowers) in Christian community. The first thing to do is place it in that context, and not in the category of marital "leftovers."

> Let not a widow be taken into the number under threescore years old, having been the wife of one man, well reported of for good works; if she have brought up children, if she have lodged strangers, if she have washed the saints' feet, if she have relieved the afflicted, if she have diligently followed every good work. (1 Tim. 5:9–16)

Women generally live longer than men do, and husbands and wives do not usually die at the same time. This means that most married women will be widowed at some point, and an important part of married life involves preparation for this. Preparation involves the widow herself, the immediate family, the extended family, and the church. In the above passage, we see that the word *widow* has two meanings, just as the word *elder* does. The word *elder* means an older person, but it also refers to someone who holds a particular office, however old they are. In the same way, a widow is a woman who has lost her husband, but a widow *enrolled* as such by the church has to meet certain qualifications for the office of widowhood. Some of this certainly reflects the conditions of the first century, but we also should not be too quick to say that none of it applies today.

In order to be enrolled, a widow had to be sixty years old and had to have been married only once (v. 9). She needed to have a good domestic reputation for good works, childrearing, hospitality, relieving the afflicted, and diligence to pursue every good work (v. 10). Younger widows are excluded because they will be tempted to marry, which would involve wantonness against Christ (v. 11), and this would be tantamount to apostasy (v. 12). Enrolling young women sets them up for a host of bad habits, encouraging them to become gossipy idlers (v. 13). So St. Paul encourages them to marry (v. 14). This would exclude them from being enrolled as a widow later because they had been married more than once. This counsel was based on bad experience (v. 15). And if any man or woman with means is related to a widow, they should be first to care for them (v. 16).

We might think of these widows as Protestant nuns. As best I can make out, the early church enrolled widows (of a certain character) who were over the age of sixty, and the church expected ministerial service from them. If they departed from this service into idleness, it was a disgrace. If they married again, this was counted as unfaithfulness to Christ, which indicated that they were bound by some kind of vow to Him to not marry again. There is something here to make both Protestants and Roman Catholics unhappy—Protestants because I have used the word *nun*, and Catholics because the qualifications for being such a nun are clean contrary to the institution they have set up.

As for the word, it just comes from medieval Latin—*nunnus*, a term of respect for older men, and *nunna,* a term of respect for older women. This use fits very well with what was going on in the first century. But note that St. Paul was actively discouraging such enrollments, and note also what the qualifications were in order to be installed in this office.

In this text, St. Paul recommends the younger widows to marry again. We must not absolutize marriage for the sake of consoling a widow or widower. Jesus says that in the resurrection, we will not marry or be given in marriage (Lk. 20:34–36). At the same time, do not conclude from this that your relationship with your spouse in the resurrection will somehow be less than what it is now. When you have "been there ten thousand years, bright shining as the sun," you will not run into your husband on the golden streets some place, and say, "Oh, hi. It's you." Whatever God has in store for us, it will be glorious beyond all mortal reckoning—but if it is just like here, then the question of the Sadducees stands (Mt. 22:23–28).

Now if a lifetime of marital faithfulness (described in detail) was required in order to bring a woman onto the rolls of the church, then this sets the general pattern for all of us as we prepare for possible separation from a spouse by death. This is the example with regard to character, whether or not a particular choice is then made. So here is the principle: you are where you went. You reap what you sow. What you invest in matters. Consider the example of Dorcas: "Then Peter arose and went with them. When he was come, they brought him into the upper chamber: and all the widows stood by him weeping, and shewing the coats and garments which Dorcas made, while she was with them" (Acts 9:39). We ought not to be distracted by the garments; we tend to look at the coats and garments she made, all of which are long gone. Look rather at the impact this woman had on the other women. The woman described here is one who invested in people, and this is what it means to prepare. The best preparation for godly responses to future circumstances (including widowhood) is cultivating godly responses to present circumstances. Those godly responses for a wife include a life of faithful lovemaking with her husband; diligence in good works; cheerfulness in the midst of diapers, runny noses, and spankings; hospitality to others; and works of mercy to the afflicted. Give and it will be given. Mercy to the afflicted is the best way to prepare for the day of your affliction.

The Lord Jesus tells us not to lay up treasures on earth, where moth and rust destroy, and where thieves break in and steal (Mt. 6:19). The Bible tells us to lay up treasure in the permanent things. Now, what are those permanent things? You are in the presence of two of them right now—they are the Word of God, and your neighbor. The grass withers and the flower fades, but the Word of the Lord lasts forever (1 Pet. 1:24–25). It follows that you should invest in the Word of God—lay up your treasure there. And your neighbor, the one right next to you, will also live forever (Jn. 5:28–29). The widows who admired the labors of Dorcas are still alive. Dorcas is still alive, in communion with the Lord Jesus in heaven—and she has the honor she does because she labored in the transient things in order to be kind in the permanent things.

CHAPTER 23

Designed to Be Sexual

What does it mean to be pro-marriage, pro-family, or pro-life? In common parlance, we know what such phrases refer to, but even here we must be careful. The basic Christian duty is to be *pro-God* and align everything else in accordance with this. When we absolutize things like "life," "marriage," or "family," we routinely get into trouble. When John the Baptist confronted Herod, he was not being pro-marriage, but rather anti-marriage (Mt. 14:4). So, let's see what God has to say about marriage and family:

> And did not he make one? Yet had he the residue of the spirit. And wherefore one? That he might seek a godly seed. Therefore take heed to your spirit, and let none deal treacherously against the wife of his youth. (Mal. 2:15)

What was God looking for when He made man and woman one? In addressing this question, we want to make sure that we do not fall into the trap of thinking that a correct answer to this question is the only possible correct answer. Marriage is not a simple thing, and the Scriptures teach that marriage extends into all the circumstances and aspects of life. Marriage goes wherever people do and is involved in whatever people are involved in. This said, God made man and woman one because He was seeking godly seed. One of the purposes of godly marriage is godly off-spring, but as we shall see, more is involved in this than simply begetting them.

This brings us to the vexed question of family planning, and the questions surrounding family planning are nuts-and-bolts questions indeed. If we want to live as faithful Christians, though, it is most necessary to address them straight up. And though it is important for all of us, it is particularly important for engaged and newly-married couples. What then are the basic biblical principles we must be committed then?

1. Children are a blessing from God (Ps. 127). Consequently, it is the responsibility of the church to create a community where couples feel free to receive this blessing from the hand of God, whether in large or small doses.

2. The Bible says nothing about birth control considered as such. I would put a reference here, but there aren't any. Where the Bible is silent, we must be silent. To legislate where God has not spoken is perilous (Deut. 4:2).

3. We are surrounded by an unbelieving culture that is hostile to the biblical vision for fruitfulness. As we make the decisions we have the liberty to make, we must take care that our motives are right, and that we are not being shaped by the secular world around us (Rom. 12:1–2).

4. Children are not an automatic blessing from God. Samuel would not have been more greatly blessed if he had seven sons who took bribes instead of two. In our text, God was seeking godly seed. As it turns out, there is a particular kind of legalistic melon-headedness that refuses to see that God has not spoken about something, and this mentality is usually ill-suited to the task of rearing godly children in wisdom. God did not call us to be mere breeders of covenant-breakers, but rather godly mothers and fathers of godly seed.

5. We are called to mind our own business (Rom. 14:12–13). If another couple is childless, you do not know if they are using birth control or not. You do not usually even have the right to care. If another couple is having lots of children, you don't know the circumstances there either. The great Pauline principle is one for the ages—mind thine own beeswax.

God calls us to wise dominion. When we plan anything, the question we must ask and answer constantly is "By what standard?" We make decisions within the boundaries of God's express word, but within those boundaries, there are two great operative principles.

The first is that we do not know the decrees of God. Therefore, all our plans and planning must be surrendered to Him at the foundational level, constantly. "Whereas ye know not what shall be on the morrow. For what is your life? It is even a vapour, that appeareth for a little time, and then vanisheth away. For that ye ought to say, If the Lord will, we shall live, and do this, or that" (Jas. 4:14–15).

The second is that "if the Lord wills" is not the same as a *que sera sera* fatalism. The triune God who predestines all things has commanded us to order our lives in accordance with the principles of means and ends, sowing and reaping, planning and executing. Because God is sovereign, our work is not absolute, but God regularly and routinely condescends to use it. There is foolish planning (Prov. 14:12), and there is wise planning. "Through wisdom is an house builded; and by understanding it is established" (Prov. 24:3); "Be thou diligent to know the state of thy flocks, and look well to thy herds" (Prov. 27:23).

This said, here are some questions to ask. As you seek to be faithful stewards in bringing up godly seed, there has to be a fundamental openness to God's veto. If you are using birth control, are you open to the gift of a new life? If you are not using birth control, are you open to God not giving children? Make your determinations in the palm of an open hand—so the Lord can give, the Lord can take away; blessed be the name of the Lord. If you are clutching something, then God needs to break your fingers to get at it.

So what are your gifts? What are your abilities? What are your financial resources? What are your financial resources likely to be ten years from now? What is your level of education? How old are you? How expensive is Christian school? How expensive (in money and time) is home schooling? Have you received wise counsel from outsiders who know you on all these questions (2 Cor. 10:12)?

God does not dispense His blessings from a vending machine—that's an operation simple enough to understand. Wealth is a blessing, but God can bless by withholding it. Long life is a blessing, but God can bless by shortening life. Food is a blessing, but Paul learned the secret of contentment when he had none. Considering all this, we see that the only unqualified, unmixed blessing is Calvinism. Never forget the *God-ness* of God.

All this said, children received from the Lord in faith and by faith are a wonderful, textured way to exhibit how triune living goes deeper and deeper, beyond our ability to reckon. Most readers of this book are ancestors, in the determination of God, to hundreds of thousands of souls yet unborn. Now *there* is a head-bender.

So one reason for sexual relations is the propagation of godly offspring. When a man leaves his father and mother and takes a wife, one of the purposes God had for this was the creation and nurture of godly seed. But as we noted at the beginning, there are more reasons for sex than simple reproduction. We come now to consider the purposes of marriage in a fallen world, and one of them is sexual protection against immorality:

> Nevertheless, to avoid fornication, let every man have his own wife, and let every woman have her own husband. Let the husband render unto the wife due benevolence: and likewise also the wife unto the husband. The wife hath not power of her own body, but the husband: and likewise also the husband hath not power of his own body, but the wife. Defraud ye not one the other, except it be with consent for a time, that ye may give yourselves to fasting and prayer; and come together again, that Satan tempt you not for your incontinency. But I speak this by permission, and not of commandment. (1 Cor. 7:2–6)

Paul had advised the Corinthian Christians against marriage for the time being. He did this because of the "present distress" (1 Cor. 7:26–29). It is one thing to deny Christ or they throw you to the lions, and quite another to deny Christ or they throw your wife and children to the lions. Paul wanted the Christians of his generation to "travel light." Even so, certain things were more important, sexual purity among them. One of the purposes of marriage is to avoid fornication, and this valuable function is provided for both sexes (v. 2). But just getting married will not result in this unless the privilege is used (v. 3). Paul begins with mutual benevolence (v. 3) and moves on to the exercise of authority (v. 4). Both the husband and wife are called to give, and both are given permission to require. To live in any other way is identified by Paul as a species of fraud (v. 5). A short time of sexual abstinence in marriage is permissible (v. 5), but only for a time and with mutual consent (v. 6).

This kind of hard-headed pastoral advice conflicts with some forms of sentimental romanticism. Some people are likely to feel "used"—they might object that this makes the Christian approach to sexual relations sound like a question of mere duty and pragmatic quenching of biological desire, rather than the natural result of soaring heights of emotional and spontaneous feelings for one another. Well, yes. Although we might quarrel with the use of words like *mere* to describe this, we have to remember that we live in the world God made, and not in the fictional worlds we have sometimes sought to make for ourselves.

Now of course there is a way that some people have of "using" others that is morally reprehensible, but let us not get overly scrupulous: "For this cause God gave them up unto vile affections: for even their women did change the natural use into that which is against nature: And likewise also the men, leaving the natural use of the woman, burned in their lust one toward another; men with men working that which is unseemly, and receiving in themselves that recompense of their error which was meet" (Rom. 1:26–27). When we use one another in a way contrary to God's law, the end result is that we use one another up. But when we remember the natural use of the woman, and the natural use of the man, the results are usually very pleasant. All of this is in the context of love, which is the summary of the law and the prophets.

This is a blessing for both sexes. As a downstream result of some Victorian pedestal setting, a common assumption in the Christian world is that (generally speaking) men have sexual problems and that (generally speaking) women do not. Women are somehow thought to be mysteriously above it all, or at least *Christian* women are thought to be above it all. "Women are bulletproof, but guys struggle"—or so the thinking goes. But notice that, in our text, the apostle Paul does not break it out that way. The marriage bed is given to protect men and women *both* from sexual temptation, and living a certain way within marriage is designed to protect both men and women from temptation.

There is a stark difference between morality and moralism. The problem we face in the conservative church can be seen in treatments of subjects like this one. This portion of this chapter was originally a sermon preached to a congregation that had a lot of little kids there. And so we worry, "How could he talk about sex openly like this? What about the *children?*" Let us consider the question this way: Is the book of Leviticus PG-13? Is the Song of Solomon an R? What preconditions had to be fulfilled in order for *Christians* to start worrying about whether Bible passages were a good influence on their children? Furthermore, do they think that external protection will result in internal innocence? It's true that the world does not hesitate to bombard your children with lascivious thoughts, images, commercials, and suggestions, but if you successfully hide in the woods for twenty years during their upbringing, their great grandfather Adam will successfully bombard them with all the same things from within.

We are called to sexual discipleship, not sexual neutrality, fear, or diffidence. This means teaching on sexual matters. Jesus said that part of the Great Commission involved teaching obedience to everything that He taught, and He was not at all silent on this subject. We have every right to expect the church to be a moral place; we should shudder at the prospect of it becoming a moralistic place.

We are not told to keep the marriage bed pure by hiding the facts concerning it from one another or pretending that this is not a very important aspect of our humanity. We are told to keep the marriage bed pure by honoring it: "Marriage is honorable in all, and the bed undefiled: but whoremongers and adulterers God will judge" (Heb. 13:4). Further, everything is connected, which means that Scripture's teaching on sex is closely tied to its teaching on creation, glory, honor, Trinity, roles, relationships, worship, and the rest of it. If this chapter is the only part of this book that someone seeks to apply, the results will not be encouraging for him. But if these things are considered in the context of everything else, and we avoid perfectionism, we will find that God gave us the blessing of marriage for a reason. One of God's central means for helping us deal with sexual temptation is called sexual relations. There is nothing mysterious about it. This cannot be understood in isolation, but it needs to be understood.

One danger is that in discussions between husbands and wives on this subject, men usually offend (sinfully) and women are usually offended (sinfully). The two important elements to remember in preparing for the natural use of marriage are *honesty* and *honor*. Say that a husband expresses some of his sexual interests or temptations (and let us also say that he is a normal Christian guy and not a pervert), it is still possible for a wife to be offended. If that happens several times, he might just clam up.

This brings us to the third reason for sexual relations between husband and wife: union and communion.

> For we are members of his body, of his flesh, and of his bones. For this cause shall a man leave his father and mother, and shall be joined unto his wife, and they two shall be one flesh. This is a great mystery: but I speak concerning Christ and the church. (Eph. 5:30–32)

The way that husbands and wives are instructed to treat one another throughout this passage is based on Christ's love for His bride. Now Christ did not love His bride from a distance; He came to earth and was united to her, a point which Paul makes very clear in his conclusion to this passage. And though we want to speak discretely—as Paul does—we don't want to be so discrete as to miss his point. We are members of Christ's body, of His flesh and of His bones (v. 30)—we are united with Christ in a profound and mysterious way. Just when he is done with this statement, Paul cites Genesis again, speaking about a man leaving his home, being joined to his wife, and becoming one flesh with her (v. 31). We become one with Christ in a way somehow analogous to how a man and woman become sexually one. This is a great mystery, but the point is Christ and the church (v. 32).

This high theological significance of marriage has led Roman Catholics to treat marriage as a sacrament, so let us consider that point for a moment. We, being good Protestants, believe that God has appointed only two sacraments in the Church: baptism and the Lord's Supper. But this sometimes causes people to miss the point of sacraments—they were given in order to suffuse the whole of our lives (including marriage). Everywhere you go, you are baptized and bear the name of Jesus Christ; do not bear it in vain. You are also nourished by the Lord's Supper for all that you do throughout the course of the week. Moreover, many elements of the world around us are sacramental (though not sacraments proper), and they help fill out the meaning of the two sacraments. Included in this would be things like washing, eating and drinking, and sexual union. So, though there are only two sacraments, they give sacramental significance to our entire lives.

The biblical terminology in the Ephesians passage is one reason why Catholics regard marriage as a sacrament. The Latin word *sacramentum* in the Vulgate Bible is the translation of the Greek word used here, which is *mysterion*. When Paul says "mystery" here, he does not mean a detective whodunnit. It has to be on a par with, and probably related to, the great mystery of how

Jew and Gentile were brought together to have communion in Christ, and it is a great mystery. Similarly, sexual union is not simply scratching a biological itch or urge; it is a great mystery, and it was intended to be a mystery of union and communion.

So, we are of His flesh and of His bone, even as we in marriage are one flesh with our spouse. We have already considered two other purposes of the sexual union. One of them is the begetting of godly children, and we thank God for it. The second, given the presence and aggressiveness of a lust-filled world, not to mention our own remaining corruptions, is the prevention of sexual sin. We thank God for this as well. But neither of these purposes lies at the heart of what covenant marriage is. Sexual union without a covenant does not establish a marriage (1 Cor. 6:16), but a covenant of friendship or companionship without sexual union does not establish a marriage either (1 Sam. 18:3). Having said this, we need to remember everything else that St. Paul has said in this passage about honor, love, sacrifice, tenderness, and closeness. The mere fact of sexual union alone, together with the ratification of that covenant commitment at the county courthouse, will get you nothing but an ignored and despised "great mystery." What good is it to be in possession of a great mystery that you trample on?

We have addressed some of the practical considerations of our sexuality—these are purposes that lie outside the relationship itself. One is to multiply the possibility of other relationships—the countless marriages of all your descendants. The second is to protect the existing relationship from outside seduction. But—giving all glory to God—we also need to realize that sex in marriage exists for its own sake. It is self-justifying. *You don't need a reason to make love.*

Now, when all this is remembered, what are the characteristics of union and communion in marital love? What is lovemaking like when husbands are loving sacrificially and wives are honoring and respecting? Remember—meaning no disrespect—Christlikeness is not to be left outside the bedroom in the hall. This is important to recall because many Christians, for the sake of misunderstood "reverence," leave Christ out of this—and the results are consistently unhappy. But husbands and wives are to imitate Christ and His bride in their demeanor and approach to all things, including the marriage bed.

We are to desire one another, and not in an insipid, perfunctory way: "I am come into my garden, my sister, my spouse: I have gathered my myrrh with my spice; I have eaten my honeycomb with my honey; I have drunk my wine with my milk: eat, O friends; drink, yea, drink abundantly, O beloved" (Song 5:1). The verb for "drink abundantly" here means to get drunk. The Bible requires it, so you'd better do it.

Next, marital communion is an occasion for healthy wonder. What kind of God thought this up? The answer of the Christian is simple—our triune God thought this up. "There be three things which are too wonderful for me, yea, four which I know not: The way of an eagle in the air; the way of a serpent upon a rock; the way of a ship in the midst of the sea; and the way of a man with a maid" (Prov. 30:18–19). The way of a man with a maid is simply strange and wondrous.

Finally, lovemaking is just plain fun. Our Puritan fathers made much of this passage: "And it came to pass, when he had been there a long time, that Abimelech king of the Philistines looked out at a window, and saw, and, behold, Isaac was sporting with Rebekah his wife" (Gen. 26:8). Let's call this what it is—a holy horsing around.

Please be aware of the fact that many of our fathers down through church history did not have as balanced a view of the body and human sexuality as they ought to have. The most notable and striking exception to this was our Puritan fathers, who restored the biblical view. They recognized that according to Scripture, married sexuality was created by God to be exuberant. I'll conclude with a blend of some "puritanical" quotations: lovemaking should be with a "good will and delight, willingly, readily, and cheerfully," your wife is a "companion for pleasure," your passion for her should be "a golden ball of pure fire," and accompanied by "all demonstrations of hearty affection."[1] Clearly, not a few Christian marriages would greatly improve if they were more "puritanical" in this way.

---

[1] Leland Ryken, *Wordly Saints* (Grand Rapids: Zondervan, 1986), 39ff.

The sun does not get up at the same time every day. But he does get up. The sun doesn't even set at the same time every day, but we always have a sunset. Sometimes spring is early, sometimes late. Snow arrives in October one year and stays until March, but then never shows up at all, not even for Christmas, the very next year. God's world is generally predictable, but not *exactly* predictable. If the weather teaches us anything, it is that God is in charge and He does as He pleases. . . .

This has particular application in raising children. Life should be generally predictable for them. This gives them security and makes them feel loved and cared for. But the schedule should never become more important than they are. I seem to remember the Lord saying something like this: "The schedule was made for man, not man for the schedule." If keeping to the schedule is an ongoing temptation and source of friction in the home, then the schedule is a snare and a trap. If parents think they are godly if they "run a tight ship," but the children are like the Von Trapp family before Maria arrived, then all is not well. Real godliness can discern the difference between external conformity to the rules and a heart overflowing with delight in obedience. Wisdom knows when the schedule needs to be ignored, stretched, or thrown out all together.

building *her* house
commonsensical wisdom for Christian women
by nancy wilson

CPSIA information can be obtained at www.ICGtesting.com
Printed in the USA
BVOW08s1942020813

327579BV00005B/12/P

The sun does not get up at the same time every day. But he does get up. The sun doesn't even set at the same time every day, but we always have a sunset. Sometimes spring is early, sometimes late. Snow arrives in October one year and stays until March, but then never shows up at all, not even for Christmas, the very next year. God's world is generally predictable, but not *exactly* predictable. If the weather teaches us anything, it is that God is in charge and He does as He pleases. . . .

This has particular application in raising children. Life should be generally predictable for them. This gives them security and makes them feel loved and cared for. But the schedule should never become more important than they are. I seem to remember the Lord saying something like this: "The schedule was made for man, not man for the schedule." If keeping to the schedule is an ongoing temptation and source of friction in the home, then the schedule is a snare and a trap. If parents think they are godly if they "run a tight ship," but the children are like the Von Trapp family before Maria arrived, then all is not well. Real godliness can discern the difference between external conformity to the rules and a heart overflowing with delight in obedience. Wisdom knows when the schedule needs to be ignored, stretched, or thrown out all together.

building *her* house

commonsensical wisdom for Christian women

by nancy wilson

CPSIA information can be obtained at www.ICGtesting.com
Printed in the USA
BVOW08s1942020813

327579BV00005B/12/P